A biblical guide to

love, sex and marriage

A biblical guide to

love, sex and
marriage

Derek and Rosemary Thomas

 EVANGELICAL PRESS

EVANGELICAL PRESS
Faverdale North, Darlington, DL3 0PH, England

e-mail: sales@evangelicalpress.org

Evangelical Press USA
P. O. Box 825, Webster, New York 14580, USA

e-mail: usa.sales@evangelicalpress.org

web: http://www.evangelicalpress.org

First published 2007

British Library Cataloguing in Publication Data available

ISBN-13   978-0-85234-661-7   ISBN 0-85234-661-1

Printed and bound in the United States of America.

Contents

Preface

Writing this book has been a collaborative project. Though the actual writing was mine, the reservoir from which much of it was drawn is my own marriage to my wife Rosemary. As I put the finishes touches together, two landmarks were visible: our thirtieth wedding anniversary and the prospect of being grandparents.

We first met in Aberystwyth, on the west coast of Wales. It must have been September 1971, though I do not recall the encounter. I was then unconverted and though we both attended lectures on Pure Mathematics together, she was a member of what I then called 'The God Squad'. It was not for me! But God had other plans and by December I had been soundly converted, my eyes opened to see beauties hitherto unseen — including a young girl from Belfast!

It was not 'love at first sight'. At least, that was my experience. Rosemary tells it differently! What began as Christian friendship grew to something more. We lived in halls less than a hundred yards apart, attending almost the same lectures (I majored in Applied Mathematics, but took many 'Pure' courses, too), worshipped at the same church (Alfred Place Baptist Church where the minister was, and still is, Geoff Thomas), and took an active part in the IVF University Christian Union (now UCCF). Hardly a day went by when we didn't see each other.

Friendship grew into love, love into engagement and engagement into marriage. In the space of two years, our companionship had become a commitment to be faithful to each other 'in plenty and in want, in joy and in sorrow ... till death do us part'. We were married in Aberystwyth, the church that we had grown to love, on 31 July 1976. To the strains of Bach's 'Jesu, joy of man's desiring', Rosemary walked down the aisle, accompanied by her father, and we were joined together as husband and wife. And so began an adventure...

Time flies, as they say. It hardly seems possible that thirty years have passed by. We have had our joys and sorrows — to be honest, more joy than sorrow. Two extraordinary children filled our lives with adventure and responsibility. They have enriched our marriage in ways we could not possibly calculate. Typical family memories of vacations, Christmas, birthdays, school events, particular triumphs *and tragedies* fill our minds and are ritually remembered on those occasions when we gather as a family.

As our thirtieth wedding anniversary came, I wrote these words on the church blog site:

Rosemary,

Have I told you that you're the only girl I ever kissed? Yes, I know I have! Many times! Well, I've kissed a few ladies old enough to be my mother, but that's not the same! You were, and remain, the only one I wanted to marry and grow old with. But even that's not turning out as I thought since I'm the one that's growing old, and you seem to get younger! Why is it that men turn ugly and women grow more beautiful? It doesn't seem quite fair to me, but since I don't look at myself too much, I think I win out on this one.

It was thirty years ago I said 'I will' and 'I do' and 'Till death us do part'. I remember every minute of it. The organist had only played about five bars of 'Jesu, joy of man's desiring' and you were right there — radiant!

I never thought marriage would be so much fun! No one told me it would get better and better, but it does.

President Ronald Reagan wrote to the First Lady, on his 31st anniversary, 'I told you once it was like an adolescent's dream of what a marriage should be like. That hasn't changed.' I can say the same.

You make me look far better than I am.

You never stop loving our children ('fussing over them' as I often say, 'like a broody hen').

The Lord has given me in you a treasure, that I in no way deserve.

As we await our first grandchild, these are the words in my heart: 'Many women have done excellently, but you surpass them all' (Proverbs 31:29).

Books are often collaborative efforts. Several people have helped me, to whom I am indebted. Several student assistants, including John Tweeddale, Tony Layzell and Nick Reid, helped in proof-reading, the latter in the week before his wedding. My secretary has a keen eye for composition and spent her vacation proof-reading — surely, a work of supererogation! Most of all, the members of First Presbyterian Church in Jackson, Mississippi, gave encouragement following a series of sermons in the summer of 2004. Without their enthusiasm, and the infectious support of my friend and senior minister, Ligon Duncan, I never would have had the courage to preach on the Song of Solomon.

I mentioned earlier the prospect of being grandparents. Since first writing this, we have rejoiced over the birth of our first grandchild — a girl, Hannah May! Marriage has produced another generation. As Ellen and David, my daughter and son-in-law, continue on their latest adventure as parents, it is to them that I dedicate this book.

Derek Thomas
August 2007

Introduction

In my youth they used to make me read the Bible. Trouble was, the only books I took to naturally were the ones that they weren't over and above keen on, but I got to know the Song of Songs pretty well by heart.

('Lord Peter Wimsey',
DOROTHY SAYERS, 1893-1957)

This book is about marriage and its relationships. As we study this together, we will base much of what we say on the Song of Solomon. Interpreting this book of the Bible has been a controversial issue for many years. However, as we look at it, I have at least three things in mind.

First, it is a book about love, marriage and sex. It is thoroughly immersed in the goodness of the created order. Augustine's doctrine of *concupiscence* — which taught that original sin introduced in Adam a fundamental disorder in human sexuality that questioned the very propriety of sexual relations — is an understandable reaction to his profligate youth. Protestants and Catholics have interpreted Augustine differently (the warning given to seminary students about entering a study of Augustine and not being able to find the way out again is a very real one!). Catholicism has inherited a tendency to look with suspicion on the role sex is meant to have, insisting at times that it is a necessity merely for the purposes of procreation. The Song of Solomon has something to teach us in this respect: the joy of sexual union in a loving, monogamous relationship.

Second, in teaching us about intimate relationships in marriage, it helps us understand how marital union reflects Christ's relationship to the church corporately, and the believer individually. I will argue that this is *not* its primary intent. Nevertheless, it is a valid application of what love for Christ and by Christ means for us as believers. Not every detail of the Song can be pressed into service this way. For that reason, it will be best to refer to the relationship of the Song to union with Christ as *analogous* rather than allegorical. Even if we take the book to be illustrative of a deeper idea — the love of Jesus Christ for his bride, the church, the propriety of which Paul clearly affirms in Ephesians 5:25-27 — there must be a sense in which the primary significance lies on the surface: the love of a would-be suitor for his lover and would-be wife! It is impossible to avoid the reality of the underlying picture upon which the analogy is built. There is a prevailing romance and sexuality no matter how we go about ascertaining what the *ultimate* lesson for us may be. The love scene in chapter 4, for example, is given in a most exquisite and delicate fashion. The poetry is often subtle and sublime. It is celebrating monogamous, sexual union within the boundaries of marriage, and it does so with discretion and taste; but it also does so with romance and ongoing courtship. Only after we have seen its primary intent as illustrative of sexual passion within the loving covenant of marriage can we then explore what this might have to say of our love for Christ and more especially of his love for us.

Third, the Song of Solomon is God's inerrant Word. It is breathed out by God and 'profitable for teaching, for reproof, for correction, and for training in righteousness, that the man of God may be competent, equipped for every good work' (2 Timothy 3:16-17). We cannot keep this issue buried beneath the surface; it must hover over everything we understand of the Song. Being persuaded of its divine authorship and sanctifying intent should keep us from embarrassment on the one hand and sentimentality on the other. The Holy Spirit thought it necessary that we be given these love poems to teach and exhort us to love more deeply the one he has provided to share our lives with. It is only right, therefore, that we reciprocate with gratitude for this gift.

It is time to read a little poetry!

Song of Solomon 1:1 - 2:7

1   *The Song of Songs, which is Solomon's.*

SHE

2   *Let him kiss me with the kisses of his mouth!*
     For your love is better than wine;
3   *your anointing oils are fragrant;*
     your name is oil poured out;
      therefore virgins love you.
4   *Draw me after you; let us run.*
      The king has brought me into his chambers.

OTHERS

We will exult and rejoice in you;
     we will extol your love more than wine;
     rightly do they love you.

SHE

5   *I am very dark, but lovely,*
      O daughters of Jerusalem,
     like the tents of Kedar,
      like the curtains of Solomon.

6   *Do not gaze at me because I am dark,*
      because the sun has looked upon me.
   My mother's sons were angry with me;
      they made me keeper of the vineyards,
      but my own vineyard I have not kept!
7   *Tell me, you whom my soul loves,*
      where you pasture your flock,
      where you make it lie down at noon;
   for why should I be like one who veils herself
      beside the flocks of your companions?

HE

8   *If you do not know,*
      O most beautiful among women,
   follow in the tracks of the flock,
      and pasture your young goats
      beside the shepherds' tents.

9   *I compare you, my love,*
      to a mare among Pharaoh's chariots.
10   *Your cheeks are lovely with ornaments,*
      your neck with strings of jewels.

OTHERS

11   *We will make for you ornaments of gold,*
      studded with silver.

SHE

12   *While the king was on his couch,*
      my nard gave forth its fragrance.
13   *My beloved is to me a sachet of myrrh*
      that lies between my breasts.
14   *My beloved is to me a cluster of henna blossoms*
      in the vineyards of Engedi.

15   *Behold, you are beautiful, my love;*
      behold, you are beautiful;
      your eyes are doves.

16   *Behold, you are beautiful, my beloved, truly delightful.*
    Our couch is green;
17   *the beams of our house are cedar;*
      our rafters are pine.

2

  I am a rose of Sharon,
  a lily of the valleys.

2   *As a lily among brambles,*
    so is my love among the young women.

3   *As an apple tree among the trees of the forest,*
    so is my beloved among the young men.
  With great delight I sat in his shadow,
    and his fruit was sweet to my taste,
4   *He brought me to the banqueting house,*
    and his banner over me was love.
5   *Sustain me with raisins;*
    refresh me with apples,
    for I am sick with love.
6   *His left hand is under my head,*
    and his right hand embraces me!
7   *I adjure you, O daughters of Jerusalem,*
    by the gazelles or the does of the field,
  that you not stir up or awaken love
    until it pleases.

1.

Love's beginning

First time he kissed me, he but only kissed
The finger of this hand wherewith I write;
And ever since, it grew more clean and white...
The third upon my lips was folded down
In perfect, purple state; since when, indeed,
I have been proud and said, 'My love, my own.'
ELIZABETH BARRETT BROWNING (1806-61)

The Song of Solomon is a series of songs — love songs. *Canticum canticorum* is its Latin title, and is the reason why, in older commentaries and especially Puritan sermons, it is referred to as *Canticles*, 'a song'.

The first song (1:1 - 2:7) is composed of a series of five 'snapshots' in which we are introduced to two *principal* characters. There also seems to be a third — a group of women of Jerusalem who speak collectively as a single unit. They are probably unmarried friends of the principal female character.

Beauty and the eye of the beholder

In the first snapshot, the chapter begins with a young country girl who has glimpsed a handsome prince, a young man she has come to know, though she does not identify him for us in this chapter. In verse 2, the woman speaks of the one she loves, 'Let him kiss me with the kisses of his mouth!'

She has fallen in love with an attractive young man! And she desires to be with him. The physical attraction seems to have emerged from previous encounters. Evidently others have found him equally attractive (1:4).

She wants to be kissed by him! What girl doesn't want to be kissed! What young man doesn't! This is the language of love, the poetry of dreams. There's romance in the air. There's nothing amiss here. There is no need to apply 'twenty-five rules of courtship' just yet. That will come later!

Though her attraction to him is initially expressed in physical terms, it moves into something more objective — his character, his name, his reputation, his standing before others, and his spiritual side. She exclaims, 'Your anointing oils are fragrant; your name is oil poured out; therefore virgins love you' (v. 3). This is more than infatuation, more than momentary lust. There has been some investigation of background, of character. Everybody knew his character. Everybody likes this man. He has a standing. He has a good reputation. He is what a friend of mine calls euphemistically, M & M: 'marriage material'!

There is something about him that this young lady likes; she calls him 'oil poured out'. This means more than that he simply smelled good, although that was probably an important consideration in days when deodorant had yet to be discovered! No doubt the use of various oils in their ablutions covered a multitude of sins!

There is more, then, than chemistry at work here. There is character — character she respects. Lasting relationships will

19

survive on character not physical attraction for the obvious reason that youthful beauty is a fleeting commodity. There is no good engaging in a relationship with someone you do not respect, no matter how physically attractive they may be. No good will come of it. He may be, let's say, 6'2'' and 175 pounds, have green eyes, a great body and make a bundle of money. He may even drive a Porsche! Yes, and hell may come along with a relationship! It is better to say,

'I want someone who loves God more than he loves me.'
'I want someone with a servant's heart.'
'I want someone whom my friends see as a man of standing and godly character.'

It is all very well to fall in love with a hunk, but you have to ask, 'A hunk of what?'

Tanned

In verses 5 and 6, we see the second snapshot and discover an example of how we need to be contextual when reading the Song of Solomon — or any section of Scripture! Apparently, folk were expressing opinions about the fact that she was tanned from overexposure to the sun! She explains what she means: 'I am very dark, but lovely... Do not gaze at me because I am dark, because the sun has looked upon me.' A tan was not a good thing in those days. How times have changed!

She also speaks about her mother's sons — maybe stepbrothers — making her work. She was forced into the fields to labour, and as a result her skin was dark. Evidently, life was hard for this young girl. She has suffered a little. In contrast to the seeming attractiveness of the young man, this girl, on the surface at least, is not such a great catch! Undoubtedly this is her own estimation of herself, making her lover seem better than her. Perhaps this was part of the attraction he saw in her — a sense of humility that might today seem to border on low self-esteem; but to this man it was evidence of another character trait: a servant's heart!

She wants to meet him again. 'Tell me,' she asks, 'you whom my soul loves, where you pasture your flock, where you make it lie down at noon; for why should I be like one who veils herself beside the flocks of your companions?' (1:7). But where is he? The young man she loves is a shepherd! He'll be in one of those locations where his flocks rest from the noon-day sun, that's where! But if she comes with a veil on her face at noon, she might be mistaken for a prostitute. It's all about appearances and proprieties. She wants to do the right thing; she doesn't want to act in an inappropriate way. She is eager to set a good reputation about herself, too. As much as she longs for him, she doesn't want to throw herself at him.

A mare amongst stallions

In verses 8-11, when the man is speaking to the woman, he likens her to a horse! 'I compare you, my love, to a mare among Pharaoh's chariots' (v. 9). The language of love has changed since the days of Solomon — nowadays, to liken a woman to a horse is inadvisable unless she happens to be 'the horsey type'. Even then, it is probably not going to sound endearing. But here, it is meant to be a compliment!

Again, we need to know a little context. He is likening her to an Egyptian horse, and Egyptian horses, apparently, were the best in the world; and she is a mare amongst stallions. In Egypt, chariots were usually pulled by stallions. And in order to defeat an enemy coming at you with horses — stallions and chariots — you could place a mare in amongst them and it would drive the stallions wild. Maybe that is what he means. She drives him wild! We're not through the first chapter and things are getting a little hot!

Eyes only for you

The scene changes again in verses 12-14, and we find another snapshot. The woman is at a banquet filled with many people. There is eating and drinking. And talking!

But, she has eyes only for him.

She is wearing a pouch filled with myrrh that gives off fragrance. 'While the king was on his couch, my nard gave forth its fragrance. My beloved is to me a sachet of myrrh that lies between my breasts' (vv. 12-13). This is the language of aromatherapy! She imagines that instead of this pouch hanging between her breasts the head of her lover might be there.

Cyril of Alexandria thought the two breasts were the Old and New Testament, and that the one lying between them was Jesus! But that is to miss the point, don't you think? She is imagining him as her husband, that she will one day marry him. Remember, this is a song of love about him and about her. She desires to be with him.

To her, 'My beloved is to me a cluster of henna blossoms in the vineyards of Engedi' (v. 14). Engedi is an oasis in the desert, in the wasteland. Even today, if you tour Israel and go to Engedi, all of a sudden you see blossom and fruit. The ancient prophesies of the desert blossoming like a rose have come true through modern irrigation techniques.

Under the apple tree

Finally, we see the fifth picture. The two are alone, walking in the country, and resting under an apple tree. They are looking at each other; their eyes are locked in each other's gaze. And he says to her, 'Behold, you are beautiful, my love; behold, you are beautiful; your eyes are doves' (v. 15).

She responds to him, 'Behold, you are beautiful, my beloved, truly delightful' (v. 16).

They have fallen in love, and they are telling each other so. These are not the furtive glances of the earlier pictures that sent their hearts racing. This is much more intense than that!

In 2:1, the woman says something about herself that is interesting, 'I am a rose of Sharon, a lily of the valleys.' Did you note the change that has taken place from chapter 1? In chapter 1, she is unsure of herself. She is unsure of her looks, her demeanour; she's tanned and not sure whether he is going to like her, but now, all of a sudden, there is self-confidence. So, what has happened?

Love! The love of someone she deeply cares for. It has changed her perception of herself and given her worth, value. This is what love has done for her. She has begun to see herself as one who is loved and cherished, and that makes all the difference in the world.

Those of us who are married know this experience well. We are amazed every day that someone should say they want to spend the rest of their lives with us — and they know us! And they are still saying, 'I want to spend the rest of my life with you; I want to grow old with you; I want to share my stories with you; I want to wake up in the morning and talk to you.'

This is what has happened here; she *knows* that he loves her.

'This bud of love by summer's ripening breath may prove to be a beauteous flower when next we meet,' Shakespeare says in *Romeo and Juliet*. And this is precisely what is in view here, in the Romeo and Juliet of the Bible — the Song of Solomon.

Charles Williams, fellow member of The Inklings, along with C. S. Lewis and J. R. R. Tolkien, wrote that, when we love someone, we see their eternal identity, 'the mode of expansion of one moment into eternity'.[1] There is something to that, and we see it in these verses. When you love someone, all the defects of that individual seem to go to the side. You know they are there, of course; love isn't totally blind. You know the faults, and sometime the faults come into focus and have to be dealt with. But when you truly love someone, you forgive them their faults because you see something deeper, something eternal.

> ...when I approach
> Her loveliness, so absolute she seems
> And in herself complete, so well to know
> Her own, that what she wills to do or say
> Seems wisest, virtuousest, discreetest, best.
> All higher knowledge in her presence falls
> Degraded.
>
> (John Milton, *Paradise Lost, Book 7*)

This is the language of romance, of love.

Nothing spells true servanthood better than love. The engaging of our affections in a love for someone other than ourselves is what being a servant is about.

We see this exemplified in Jesus when he denied himself, became a man and entered into this world to redeem his people from their sins. He, too, saw our sins — better than we will ever see them! And still he loved us.

'What did he see in us?' we ask, as though some answer should be forthcoming that might give some reasonableness for the extravagance showed us at Calvary. But none is forthcoming.

He loved us — when we were *unlovely*.

Song of Solomon 2:8 - 3:5

SHE

8 *The voice of my beloved!*
   Behold, he comes,
   leaping over the mountains,
   bounding over the hills.
9 *My beloved is like a gazelle*
   or a young stag.
   Behold, there he stands
   behind our wall,
   gazing through the windows,
   looking through the lattice.
10 *My beloved speaks and says to me:*
   'Arise, my love, my beautiful one,
   and come away,
11 *for behold, the winter is past;*
   the rain is over and gone.
12 *The flowers appear on the earth,*
   the time of singing has come,
   and the voice of the turtledove
   is heard in our land.

13   *The fig tree ripens its figs,*
        and the vines are in blossom;
        they give forth fragrance.
    Arise, my love, my beautiful one,
        and come away.

14   *O my dove, in the clefts of the rock,*
        in the crannies of the cliff,
    let me see your face,
        let me hear your voice,
    for your voice is sweet,
        and your face is lovely.

15   *Catch the foxes for us,*
        the little foxes
    that spoil the vineyards,
        for our vineyards are in blossom.'

16   *My beloved is mine, and I am his;*
        he grazes among the lilies.

17   *Until the day breathes*
        and the shadows flee,
    turn, my beloved, be like a gazelle
        or a young stag on cleft mountains.

3   *On my bed by night*
    I sought him whom my soul loves;
        I sought him, but found him not.

2   *I will rise now and go about the city,*
        in the streets and in the squares;
    I will seek him whom my soul loves.
        I sought him, but found him not.

3   *The watchmen found me*
        as they went about in the city.
    'Have you seen him whom my soul loves?'

4   *Scarcely had I passed them*
        when I found him whom my soul loves.
    I held him, and would not let him go
        until I had brought him into my mother's house,
        and into the chamber of her who conceived me.
5   *I adjure you, O daughters of Jerusalem,*
        by the gazelles or the does of the field,
    that you not stir up or awaken love
        until it pleases.

2.

A time to embrace – finding a partner

And the stars were shining...
    The earth smelt sweet...
The garden gate creaked...
And a footstep brushed the sand.
    She entered, fragrant,
    And fell into my arms.
O soft kisses, tender caresses,
    While I, all a-quiver,
    Unveiled her lovely features!
Vanished for ever is my dream of love...
    The time has fled
    And I die in despair.
Never have I loved life so deeply!
                        'Tosca', GIACOMO PUCCINI [1858–1924]

Because the Song of Solomon is one of the wisdom books of the Bible, its function is to help us live lives that are pleasing to God. The sage in the book of Ecclesiastes tells us that there is 'a time to embrace, and a time to refrain from embracing' (Ecclesiastes 3:5). And the question that arises in this chapter is a simple one: 'How can I know that the time for embracing has come?' Or, to put it another way, 'How do I get from where I am now to the place where I can embrace?'

This is not an easy question to answer, even though it has been asked by almost everyone at some point in their lives. The principal difficulty arises because we do not live in the same society and culture described by the Song of Solomon!

This is an issue that affects us no matter which part of the Bible we trying to understand. But when we are dealing with issues of the heart, it is all too easy to lose sight of the necessary cultural accommodations that have to be made in order to fully understand what is being described. In Bible times generally, but especially in the days when the Song of Solomon was written — the tenth century B.C. according to tradition, though some argue for a later date — the answer to the question of who is to be my life-partner would be very different.

By and large, in those days, how you moved from a single person to a married person was determined by your parents or guardians. The idea of arranged marriages may send shivers down the spine, but many of us can look back and be thankful for the wisdom and experience of parents who intervened when the emotional upheaval of their children threatened a union that spelled disaster. At the very least, parents who love their children and know the personalities of their children better than anyone can have an instinct for a marriage that will work well, and one that will not.

Lifelong relationships

Hebrew poetry often uses a stylistic formula which we might call 'book-ends'. The poem begins and ends with a reference to 'the daughters of Jerusalem'. They are, apparently, a group of young women, friends of the woman in the Song perhaps, who live in Jerusalem.

'I adjure you, O daughters of Jerusalem,
    by the gazelles or the does of the field,
that you not stir up or awaken love
    until it pleases'

(2:7; 3:5).

This is very good advice to someone as emotionally charged as this young woman appears to be. Love, or 'being in love' as we tend to say, makes us lose touch with reality. When the blood is hot, danger looms. And this young girl is apparently aware of it and warning her friends of the danger of playing with fire!

There are several things that are worth reflecting upon before we examine exactly what is said by way of warning in this poem. We must learn to trust God's providence. This is a fundamental lesson taught throughout Scripture: God provides good things for his children (cf. Proverbs 3:5-6; Matthew 6:25-34). From food, drink and raiment, the way we learn to prepare ourselves to spend our lives with someone else is to trust in the provision of Almighty God. This is the theme of this young woman, and she seems to turn to it again and again in the course of Song of Solomon (cf. 2:7; 3:5; 5:8; 8:4). She seems to be saying to these daughters of Jerusalem — single women with perhaps no immediate prospect of a young man — *Be patient and trust in God*.

She gives them counsel from her own experience. Do not 'stir up or awaken love until it pleases'. This statement is practical and full of wisdom, for to play with love is to play with fire. In other words, to run ahead of God's providence, to second-guess God, is a very dangerous thing. This young woman is giving her friends wise and godly counsel: 'Do not awaken love until the time is ready, until God has provided, and until all of the circumstances have come together. Don't play with love! Don't awaken it!'

Second, this young woman seems to be saying, 'You will need to take the long-term view of things.' This perspective about a relationship is important because the commitment of marriage is a commitment that lasts as long as you live — it may last 20, 30, or even 70 years! In marriage you will company with one person day and night, and in a world in which we are encouraged to do the very opposite, namely, to take the short-term view of things, to take the view of a few years or perhaps a few months or even one night, and to take the gains of one night as opposed to a lifetime view, this young woman is giving sound and solid advice. She is saying, 'Don't play with love until love is ready, until the circumstances are ready, until providence has come together. Don't look at just one day or one month or one year; think of a lifetime.'

If you seek short-term profits in a relationship, you are in real danger. It is a bit like what the book of Proverbs says, albeit from a masculine point of view, which in large part is the advice of a father to a son, but can be reversed without any difficulty whatsoever: 'A continual dripping on a rainy day and a quarrelsome wife are alike' (Proverbs 27:15); 'It is better to live in a corner of the housetop than in a house shared with a quarrelsome wife' (21:9).

Do you see what the writer of Proverbs is saying? When you enter into a marriage relationship, be prepared for the consequences. Though the short-term view of a relationship may entice you, you must take account of the long-term view, because you will spend the rest of your life with this person. This young woman is telling her friends not to awaken love too soon. She is trying to keep these other women from making a terrible decision — a decision with enormous consequences. It is better to struggle now than to have a lifetime of regret. She is saying that it is better to wrestle now than realize later when it is too late! It is a poor choice if you discover afterwards that the one to whom you have committed yourself is unable to help you *grow* in the Lord. In New Testament terms, she seems to be stating, 'I would rather have what Christ gives and what Christ holds than to enter a life that brings barrenness and fruitlessness.' This is a matter of trusting God, of waiting on his providence. This is how you prepare yourself for marriage.

Young men, young women, and maybe not so young men and women, are you struggling in this area? Take heed to this young women's advice, do 'not stir up or awaken love until it pleases'. Do not attempt to run ahead of the Lord's providence, but wait upon him. The Lord will provide.

How do I decide?

The second question is a difficult one. How do I decide whether this man or this woman is the very person God has for me? How did this young woman know that this young man, with whom she seems to be head over heels in love, was the right man for her? There are several principles I want to try to tease out of this passage, plus one or two other points that may be helpful.

First, lifelong companionship in marriage is not for everyone. We need to be clear; God gives to some Christians the gift of singleness in order to enable them to commit their lives in the service of Jesus Christ in a way that married folk cannot. They are free from some of the responsibilities that encompass marriage, they are able to give themselves without any reservation to the service of God, and such people are to be treasured. And they are not to be teased. We do a disservice when we constantly tease people who are not married, as though there is something wrong with them, as though they are second-class Christians. God has so ordered their lives to be single, and we need to respect that. Churches often transgress at this point and do those who are single a disservice.

A time to embrace — finding a partner

Some find themselves in a state of singleness by a deliberate choice, perhaps by a vow they have taken or because that is what they have discerned God's providence to be for them. But others find themselves in that position reluctantly and are chafing at the bit to be in a relationship. If you are in that latter category, then listen to the counsel of this young woman. Wait on the providence of God.

The second principle we need to mention is that it is perfectly healthy and biblical to want and to need the companionship of another. The woman says in 2:3: 'As an apple tree among the trees of the forest, so is my beloved among the young men. With great delight I sat in his shadow, and his fruit was sweet to my taste.' She is deeply in love. We are told in the opening chapters of Scripture, 'it is not good that the man should be alone' (Genesis 2:18). Matthew Henry wonderfully comments on this particular chapter of Genesis stating,

> [God made woman out of man]; not made out of his head to rule over him, nor out of his feet to be trampled upon by him, but out of his side to be equal with him, under his arm to be protected, and near his heart to be beloved.[1]

The writer of the book of Proverbs states, 'He who finds a wife finds a good thing and obtains favour from the LORD' (Proverbs 18:22). Marriage is God's provision for us. God made men and women for each other's companionship.

Third, God's design for a man and a woman is more than simply companionship, but we must also know companionship in a physical way. Did you notice what she says in 2:4: 'He brought me to the banqueting house, and his banner over me was love.' She is saying that the one she loves is making an open declaration of love for her. There is nothing hidden about his intentions. They are open and honourable. Everyone can see them. There is nothing clandestine about this relationship;

it is not going on behind locked doors in secret motels. It is a public, open, observable relationship. His banner in the banquet hall says 'love', and he is telling everybody that he loves this girl. She is overcome by it; she is almost fainting with love. She desires love's consummation in physical form. 'His left hand is under my head, and his right hand embraces me!' (v. 6). She is beginning to think what it might be like to live and sleep with her lover. There is nothing illicit about that. She has not transgressed at this point. She is thinking about the consequences of marriage, and it is all within the context of finding a life partner and committing herself to him in marriage.

The next words in verse 7 tell us that the time is not yet. So she tells her women friends that the time for physical companionship has not yet come, though she longs for it. To you young women, do not let a young man rob you of what you want to keep for your marriage day. Young men, do not dare take away from a young woman what she wants to keep for her wedding night. Make a solemn vow that you will not transgress at this point. Men and women, if you honour God in this area, God will honour you.

Fourth, fundamental to a Christian view of marriage is that you recognize the necessity of committing yourself only to a Christian believer. The whole context of the Song of Songs, contained as it is within the Scripture as a whole, is telling us that. The relationship between this young woman and young man is a relationship of two people who are in the Lord, for as the Scriptures state, 'Do not be unequally yoked with unbelievers' (2 Corinthians 6:14).

Now in God's providence some of you were converted after you were married, and you find yourself married to someone who is not a believer and with whom you cannot share in the most intimate spiritual matters. The Scriptures have some things to say to you, especially in the epistle of Peter (cf. 1 Peter 3:1-2). But we are not talking about that situation here. We are talking about situations where you are entering a marriage and you dare not make the mistake of marrying outside the Lord.

There is a corresponding truth to the principle of not being unequally yoked. As you are drawn to an individual, it is vital for you to ask the following questions:

- Is this person going to help me grow spiritually?
- Does this person love Jesus more than me?
- Can we achieve more for the Lord as a couple than we could as individuals?

Apart from the gospel, such questions would be foolish! However, these are the kinds of questions you need to ask yourself as you think about embarking upon a lifetime in companionship with one other person.

There is one more principle that we can tease out of this passage: listen to the advice of others. In a real sense, that is what this poem is about. This young woman is giving advice to other women, and they are to heed her advice. Do not enter into a relationship, do not let a relationship blossom and flower, and do not take the relationship to its ultimate conclusion until God's providence has so ordered that you can get married. Do you see what this young woman is saying? If you awaken love prematurely, if your passions begin to grow, rationality and thought process go out of the window. So she says, 'Do not awaken love until it is ready.' From this young woman's exhortation, we learn an important principle about relationships: listen to the advice and counsel of others.

How can I be sure?

Thirdly, how can I be sure? How can I be sure that this young man or this young woman is the one for me? How can I be sure that this is the one that God has chosen for me? How can I be sure that this marriage, this union, was made in heaven? How can I be sure? There are two passages of Scripture that come to mind.

The first passage is James 1:5-8: 'If any of you lacks wisdom, let him ask God, who gives generously to all without reproach, and it will be given him. But let him ask in faith, with no doubting, for the one who doubts is like a wave of the sea that is driven and tossed by the wind. For that person must not suppose that he will receive anything from the Lord; he is a double-minded man, unstable in all his ways.' If wisdom is what you are looking for, then take your request to the Lord. Take this matter, this issue, take your life — the whole business of courtship and marriage — take it to the Lord and lay it before him in prayer. Tell him all of your problems and all of your fears and all of your anxieties and frustrations. Tell him how fragile you are, let him provide for you, let him strengthen you, let him minister to you, and let him show you the one he has chosen for you.

The other passage that comes to mind is Proverbs 3:5-6: 'Trust in the LORD with all your heart, and do not lean on your own understanding. In all your ways acknowledge him, and he will make straight your paths.' You may be reading this chapter with a burdened and heavy heart. You have promised to keep yourself pure; you want to find a partner, a companion that meets biblical requirements. You want to find someone who will help you to grow in the Lord, who will help you to use your God-given gifts to the extension of the kingdom of God. But for your commitment, you have paid a price; there has been a cost. You have taken up a cross and you have borne a price, and men have passed you by, and perhaps (if you are a man) women have passed you by. But trust in the Lord with all your heart and lean not upon your own understanding; in all of your ways acknowledge him and he will make your paths straight.

As we can see, this passage is full of practical down-to-earth common-sense wisdom. Parents, are you burdened about your children, burdened that they do not make a mistake in finding a mate, in discerning the appropriate time to embrace? Reflecting on the principles of this chapter of the Song of Solomon would be a good place to begin. Men and women, take heed to the principle that this woman is laying down. May you find the joy of a companion with whom you are head over heels in love and whom you want to spend the rest of your life embracing to the glory of God.

Song of Solomon 2:8 - 3:5

SHE

8   *The voice of my beloved!*
      Behold, he comes,
    leaping over the mountains,
      bounding over the hills.
9   *My beloved is like a gazelle*
      or a young stag.
    Behold, there he stands
      behind our wall,
    gazing through the windows,
      looking through the lattice.
10 *My beloved speaks and says to me:*
    'Arise, my love, my beautiful one,
      and come away,
11 *for behold, the winter is past;*
      the rain is over and gone.
12 *The flowers appear on the earth,*
      the time of singing has come,
    and the voice of the turtledove
      is heard in our land.

13 *The fig tree ripens its figs,*
   and the vines are in blossom;
   they give forth fragrance.
   Arise, my love, my beautiful one,
   and come away.

14 *O my dove, in the clefts of the rock,*
   in the crannies of the cliff,
   let me see your face,
   let me hear your voice,
   for your voice is sweet,
   and your face is lovely.

15 *Catch the foxes for us,*
   the little foxes
   that spoil the vineyards,
   for our vineyards are in blossom.'

16 *My beloved is mine, and I am his;*
   he grazes among the lilies.

17 *Until the day breathes*
   and the shadows flee,
   turn, my beloved, be like a gazelle
   or a young stag on cleft mountains.

3 *On my bed by night*
   I sought him whom my soul loves;
   I sought him, but found him not.

2 *I will rise now and go about the city,*
   in the streets and in the squares;
   I will seek him whom my soul loves.
   I sought him, but found him not.

3 *The watchmen found me*
   as they went about in the city.
   'Have you seen him whom my soul loves?'

4   *Scarcely had I passed them*
       when I found him whom my soul loves.
   I held him, and would not let him go
       until I had brought him into my mother's house,
       and into the chamber of her who conceived me.

5   *I adjure you, O daughters of Jerusalem,*
       by the gazelles or the does of the field,
   that you not stir up or awaken love
       until it pleases.

3.

Growing love

I hide myself within a flower
That wearing on your breast,
You, unsuspecting, wear me too —
And angels know the rest.

EMILY DICKENSON [1830–66]

Teaching the Song of Solomon in a public setting can prove difficult, even unadvisable. Why? Because parts of it are unsuitable for young children; and its contents can be emotionally upsetting for the recently divorced or widowed. Furthermore, teaching it to single men and women needs careful handling because, as the young woman in our tale constantly reminds her sisters, it is dangerous to awaken love before it is time to consummate it.

However, the Song of Solomon does not carry a warning label! In our openly promiscuous age, there is nothing in the Song of Solomon that most have not seen or heard on television, or radio, or in the papers. The church should address these issues and teach what the Bible has to say about love, sex and marriage. If the church does not deal with these matters, who will? Nevertheless, care needs to be taken in mixed audiences and perhaps some of the contents of the Song would be better explored in special settings rather than the Sunday morning service.

Despite having eight chapters, scholars suggest that the Song of Solomon is actually comprised of six poems. The first poem, which we examined in chapter one, introduced us to what, in a play, would be called the *dramatis personae*, the principal characters. They are: a young man who is described as handsome or beautiful (1:16), and a young woman who is also described as comely and beautiful (1:15). There are also some others identified — the daughters of Jerusalem (1:5; 2:7; 3:5, 10; 5:8, 16; 8:4) — who appear to be unmarried friends of the young woman to whom, especially when she gets a little aroused, she says something very dramatic and poignant and practical.

This first poem is a love poem of magnificent and intense proportions. The two, the man and woman, are yearning for intimacy — an intimacy that will only find its fulfilment within a marriage. They have expressed their love for one another, and it is interesting that throughout this book, it is the woman who is taking most of the initiative.

The first poem ended with the two of them alone and under the shade of an apple tree (2:3). She is dreaming about the man. As the poem ends, she expresses something very earnestly to the daughters of Jerusalem, 'I adjure you, O daughters of Jerusalem, by the gazelles or the does of the field, that you not stir up or awaken love until it pleases' (2:7).

Love can sometimes be 'too hot to handle', and she is warning these young, single girls to be very careful. You must learn to walk before you can run. Before kindling the flame of desire, we need to ensure that its fulfilment can be met in a way that is both lawful and fulfilling in the ultimate sense. It is all too easy to fall prey to lust and reap the consequences of guilt and shame, and worse, as a result.

The second poem is divided into two halves; the first half of the poem ends at the end of chapter two, and the second half covers the first five verses of chapter three. In the first half of the poem, the young man is pursuing the woman, and in the second half of the poem, she is pursuing him. The two halves seem to mirror each other. In approaching this section of the Song, let us ask three questions which will help us to understand what is being said.

1. What form will a relationship that ends in marriage *initially* take?
2. What form will a relationship that ends in marriage *become*?
3. What form will a relationship that ends in marriage find by way of culmination?

Springtime — the awakening

It is Spring. The flowers are blooming; the blossom is on the fig trees; the perfume and aroma of this blossom are everywhere. And, according to Lord Alfred Tennyson in his poem 'Locksley Hall':

> In the Spring a fuller crimson comes upon the robin's breast;
> In the Spring the wanton lapwing gets himself another crest;
>
> In the Spring a livelier iris changes on the burnish'd dove;
> In the Spring a young man's fancy lightly turns to thoughts of love.

Tennyson's poem is based on the love of Orion for Merope. Orion desires marriage, but Merope's father, Oenopian, King of Chios, does not give his consent. Tennyson himself, having viewed the constellation of Orion at Locksley Hall, is reminded of his own love for 'Amy' — whose father equally did not consent; Amy was a 'puppet to a father's threat, and servile to a shrewish tongue'. The course of true love never did run smooth, they say.

Spring is that time when a young man's thoughts turn to — well, if you're about to say 'sinus infections', you need to read the Song of Solomon carefully! Spring is that time when a young man's thoughts, and in this case a young woman's thoughts, turn to love. She hears his voice. She seems to love the sound of his voice. She sees him coming towards her and describes him as a gazelle leaping and skipping. 'The voice of my beloved! Behold, he comes, leaping over the mountains, bounding over the hills. My beloved is like a gazelle or a young stag' (2:8-9). These are country folk, and, evidently, this picture of a gazelle meant something enormously powerful to her. Perhaps if you substitute a sports superstar racing down the stairs and jumping into his car, you will get a clearer picture in your mind. Later she imagines him saying to her, 'O my dove, in the clefts of the rock, in the crannies of the cliff, let me see your face, let me hear your voice, for your voice is sweet, and your face is lovely' (2:14). There's physical attraction; there's chemistry here. She wants to be with him; he wants to be with her. They've seen something in each other. Even the sound of their voices excites them — that's how a relationship begins.

But their relationship moves from a physical attraction to a desire to be together. She is utterly thrilled by his approach, charmed by his voice, entranced by his invitation; she is deeply in love. *Four* times in as many verses she speaks of him as the one 'whom my soul loves' (3:1-4). Things are getting intense. As Shakespeare says in *Romeo and Juliet*, 'This bud of love by summer's ripening breast may prove a beauteous flower when next we meet.'

There's a marvellously provocative moment when the young woman is standing beside a lattice (2:9). It is not clear if it is because he cannot see her, or she cannot see him, or whether it is a combination of both — there are no words. They are both conscious that the other is there, but there is a lattice between them. This is a scene where the two are looking for each other. He knows that she knows that he is there. She is, according to him, like a dove in the crevices cooing (2:14).

There is a wonderful modesty about all of this. There is a sense of intense propriety. There is a beautiful description of the garden blossoming and smelling wonderful, and he says, 'Let me hear your voice' (2:14). They want to talk. They want those endless hours on the telephone. It is a beautiful picture of two people who want to be together. It is a courtship. They have seen in each other something that desires to be nourished. There is nothing out-of-sight, out-of-mind about this relationship — she is in love with this man, and evidently he is in love with her, too.

Jonathan Edwards, writing on the nature of true virtue, could say, 'So a man may be affected and pleased with the features in a face, when we behold a beautiful body, a lovely proportion, a beautiful harmony of features of face, delightful airs of countenance, and voice, and sweet motion and gesture; we are charmed with it. Not under the notion of a corporeal but a mental beauty.'[1] Though his philosophy of ontology is getting in the way (!), he has seen something of Sarah that he has obviously liked. He will eventually propose marriage to her — at an inordinately young age!

Spirit and chemistry

There is a sense in this poem that the young man and young woman want this relationship to grow and blossom. There is a sense of the future about their relationship. She is actually thinking of the rest of her life with this young man. This is more than dating. There is a growing relationship here that obviously begins with physical attraction and chemistry; but there is much more to it. She calls him 'my beloved' (2:9, 10, 16, 17), and the one 'whom my soul loves' (3:1-4). Every aspect of her being is in love with this man. It is not *just* physical; it is not *just* chemistry. There is a spiritual dimension to this relationship.

Taking the long-term view of things means viewing the relationship as more than just physical. The physical will change and only the deeper character — those aspects of our personality that reflect our relationship to Jesus Christ — will endure and form the true basis of what unites and keeps love alive.

This is a poem of the love between a man and a woman. It is one based on the covenant relationship that God established in the Garden of Eden between Adam and Eve that ends in marriage and a covenant that lasts until death us do part. With that in view, we need to ask, 'Can I spend the rest of my life with this person?'

'Catch the foxes for us' (2:15), she says. What is she saying? One renowned commentator and scholar on the Song of Solomon thinks that foxes here represent old age, and what she is actually saying is, 'Let's get married before we're too old to get married.' Well, perhaps, but it certainly isn't an obvious reading!

The easier interpretation is that the little foxes would come, eat the buds of the vine and spoil them. In a relationship between a young man and a young woman, there are always difficulties; there are always obstacles and tensions particularly between two people whose passions and emotions are aroused, and particularly between two people who are not terribly mature. 'Catch the little foxes,' she is saying. 'Let's work on this relationship, and work on the problems and difficulties.'

Love, sex and marriage

Do you see what she is saying? She is saying, 'I want to take the long-term view of this. I want the problems to be solved. I want the little foxes dealt with.' This is a call to commitment. This is a call for mutual resolve to overcome the problems in a relationship. Mistrust, jealousy, selfishness, pride, egoism and an unforgiving spirit can come into a relationship and spoil it. Let us catch the little foxes.

Social commentators on the church scene in the twenty-first century often note that young men do not want to commit to marriage until they have experienced more of the opportunities of freedom. In conservative churches, couples are getting married at a later age than once they did. But there is something wrong with this picture. I do not wish to be legalistic, but in this whole dating scene, there comes a point where, perhaps after two or three dates with someone, you need to ask yourself the question, 'Can I spend the rest of my life with this person?' And if you cannot answer that in the affirmative, it needs to end. Don't go out with that person any more.

Catching the little foxes is a call to commitment, to work on the relationship. No good will come of a relationship that has no end in view, no goal in sight, no sense of direction or accountability to one another. Here, in this beautiful little poem of two people in love, there is a sense of commitment, a sense of direction, a long-term perspective; they want to work on all of the little difficulties and all of the little problems.

Intimacy

Verse 16 states: 'My beloved is mine, and I am his; he grazes among the lilies.' Some translations insert the word 'flock', but this word is not in the Hebrew text. He pastures among the lilies, and the *lilies* are interpreted here by most commentators as lips. She is talking about being kissed! She is talking about

48

intimacy. She is longing here for a marital relationship, and I stress that. There is no conflict between the Song of Solomon and the rest of Scripture here. There is an assumption in the text. She is looking into her future. This hasn't taken place yet. This is in her future. This is what she dreams about with this young man with whom she is in love. She wants to be married to him, to be sexually intimate with him.

She says at the end of verse 17, 'Turn, my beloved, be like a gazelle or a young stag on cleft mountains.' This is a little euphemism, and many commentators think that this is a reference, and let me put it as delicately as I can, to the curvaceous nature of this woman. To put it in twenty-first-century language, she wants to wake up in the morning with him right beside her. That is what she is saying. When the shadows flee away in the morning, she wants him to be there. Now, if you find that offensive, I think the problem is with you. I think that is fair to say because this is a beautiful picture. There is nothing sordid, illicit or pornographic here. This is the beauty of God's gift to a man and woman in a marital relationship, coming together in intimacy and in union. She is dreaming about the intimacy of marriage; she is thinking about the union of marriage.

There is another scene in chapter 3, which is part of this same poem. She is now pursuing him, but she cannot find him. She is lying on her bed, and she is dreaming. She is walking through the streets, but she cannot find him. She is asking people in 3:3: 'Have you seen him whom my soul loves?' When she finds him, she grasps hold of him and won't let him go. She wants to take him to the room where she was conceived. 'I held him, and would not let him go until I had brought him into my mother's house, and into the chamber of her who conceived me' (3:4). She is dreaming of her wedding day.

Things are hard now. And you notice that whenever it gets like that in the Song of Solomon (v. 5), she turns immediately to the daughters of Jerusalem and says, 'Don't store up these emotions until you're ready for it.' Such emotions are only appropriate in the context of marriage and are the *blessing* of marriage. She is overcome by it all. She is almost fainting with love. 'What is that coming up from the wilderness like columns of smoke, perfumed with myrrh and frankincense?' (3:6).

Jonathan Edwards, about a year after the citation previously given, is still thinking about Sarah; she is still inordinately young. And he is writing his diary on 6 June 1725. It is at the height of their courtship, and he observed in himself, 'I am sometimes in a frame so listless that there is no other way of profitably improving time, but conversation, visiting, or recreation, or some bodily exercise.'[2] It is the way Jonathan Edwards might say, 'What I need is a cold shower.' And it is what *she* is saying to the daughters of Jerusalem. Don't arouse these passions, these emotions, until you are ready.

The Song of Solomon is a wonderful gift that God has given to us in the Bible of something that is extraordinarily beautiful.

Song of Solomon 3:6 - 5:1

HE[1]

6   *What is that coming up from the wilderness*
      like columns of smoke,
   perfumed with myrrh and frankincense,
      with all the fragrant powders of a merchant?

7   *Behold, it is the litter of Solomon!*
   Around it are sixty mighty men,
      some of the mighty men of Israel,

8   *all of them wearing swords*
      and expert in war,
   each with his sword at his thigh,
      against terror by night.

9   *King Solomon made himself a carriage*
      from the wood of Lebanon.

10 *He made its posts of silver,*
      its back of gold, its seat of purple;
   its interior was inlaid with love
      by the daughters of Jerusalem.

11 *Go out, O daughters of Zion,*
      and look upon King Solomon,

with the crown with which his mother crowned him
 on the day of his wedding,
 on the day of the gladness of his heart.

4 Behold, you are beautiful, my love,
 behold, you are beautiful!
Your eyes are doves
 behind your veil.
Your hair is like a flock of goats
 leaping down the slopes of Gilead.
2 Your teeth are like a flock of shorn ewes
 that have come up from the washing,
all of which bear twins,
 and not one among them has lost its young.
3 Your lips are like a scarlet thread,
 and your mouth is lovely.
Your cheeks are like halves of a pomegranate
 behind your veil.
4 Your neck is like the tower of David,
 built in rows of stone;
on it hang a thousand shields,
 all of them shields of warriors.
5 Your two breasts are like two fawns,
 twins of a gazelle,
 that graze among the lilies.
6 Until the day breathes
 and the shadows flee,
I will go away to the mountain of myrrh
 and the hill of frankincense.
7 You are altogether beautiful, my love;
 there is no flaw in you.
8 Come with me from Lebanon, my bride;
 come with me from Lebanon.
Depart from the peak of Amana,

from the peak of Senir and Hermon,
from the dens of lions,
    from the mountains of leopards.

9   *You have captivated my heart, my sister, my bride;*
    you have captivated my heart with one glance of
        your eyes,
    with one jewel of your necklace.

10   *How beautiful is your love, my sister, my bride!*
    How much better is your love than wine,
    and the fragrance of your oils than any spice!

11   *Your lips drip nectar, my bride;*
    honey and milk are under your tongue;
    the fragrance of your garments is like the fragrance
        of Lebanon.

12   *A garden locked is my sister, my bride,*
    a spring locked, a fountain sealed.

13   *Your shoots are an orchard of pomegranates*
    with all choicest fruits,
    henna with nard,

14   *nard and saffron, calamus and cinnamon,*
    with all trees of frankincense,
    myrrh and aloes,
        with all chief spices —

15   *a garden fountain, a well of living water,*
    and flowing streams from Lebanon.

16   *Awake, O north wind,*
    and come, O south wind!
Blow upon my garden,
    let its spices flow.

SHE

Let my beloved come to his garden,
    and eat its choicest fruits.

HE

5   *I came to my garden, my sister, my bride,*
I gathered my myrrh with my spice,
I ate my honeycomb with my honey,
I drank my wine with my milk.

OTHERS
Eat, friends, drink,
   and be drunk with love!

4.

Wedding bells

Shall I compare thee to a summer's day?
Thou art more lovely and more temperate:
WILLIAM SHAKESPEARE [1564-1616]

'Will you have this woman to be your wife?' 'Will you have this man to be your husband?' Are there more poignant words in the liturgy of life?

Weddings are beautiful occasions; at least, they should be! It is the culmination of a providence that has brought two people together — for the rest of their lives! Two people have found in each other someone with whom they can share the most intimate aspects of their lives. There has been a courtship. Love has begun to develop. They have identified in each other characteristics which they admire and want to share. They have intimated that they desire to spend the rest of their lives together, trusting that in their union they will amount to more than they currently are as individuals.

There is a beauty, a pageantry, to a wedding! The exchange of vows, the sense of occasion, the providence of God as he has brought these two people together — these fill a wedding ceremony with a sense of occasion unequalled by any other. And a wedding is what is behind the poetry of this section of the Song of Solomon.

This is some wedding! It is a *royal* wedding — with sixty groomsmen (3:7-8), this is no 'small wedding'! Sixty groomsmen dressed in military uniform, swords glinting in the sun, must have been an impressive sight. It is tempting to think that with sixty military groomsmen it would be difficult for the groom to back out of the marriage! It certainly provided a magnificent sense of occasion.

Then there's a carriage, a palanquin, a sedan chair which he has made from the trees of Lebanon, adorned with silver, gold and purple cloth (3:9-10). The guests and onlookers must have gazed with wonder at the sight.

The entire world loves a lover. Why? Because it brings out the best in him. A good wife will make any man better than he actually is; or, at least, she will make him *look* better than he actually is. Some of his finest qualities emerge — manliness, tenderness, responsibility. His mother has given to him a crown, perhaps a signal that the parents are giving their sign of approval and blessing to this wedding (3:11). The daughters of Jerusalem have been busy preparing the interior of this carriage.

Months of work have gone into the preparations. Scores of people have been busy making arrangements and planning a pageantry that will be remembered for years to come. They want it to be a special occasion. They want to remember this day. However casual and informal society has become, however much the church may have lost touch with its roots, forgetting a sense of what is appropriate for gathered ceremonies of worship, weddings still tend to be formal occasions. People still tend to dress *up* for a wedding.

God's creation plan

The marriage of one man to one woman — *not* one man to one man and *not* one woman to one woman — is God's creation plan for men and women; although some, of course, are called to a life of singleness. Sadly, it has become necessary to stress the negative. Same-sex marriage has become a dominant issue in our times, and it is necessary to point out that it is something that is utterly foreign to the Judeo-Christian world view. This is not homophobic hysteria, despite the shrill accusations made by contemporary western democracies. As they lose touch with the world view that once shaped them, these voices will undoubtedly get louder; and the church will need to be a light in a dark world.

Interestingly, there is no record here of a marriage ceremony, as such. This is the language of poetry and the historical events that lie behind these lines are not given to us. But a marriage would have taken place, of course. It is the world view that it presupposes. Marriage is revealed as God's plan in the Bible's account of creation (cf. Genesis 2:24-25).

Before it became common to write personal vows at a marriage (a practice to be discouraged!), many marriage liturgies reflected some of the beautiful liturgy of Phillip Melancthon and Martin Bucher, and especially Thomas Cranmer's input to *The Book of Common Prayer*. Hearing the words again brings to mind a flood of memories:

> Dearly beloved, we are gathered together here in the sight of God and in the face of this congregation to join together this man and this woman in holy matrimony, which is an honourable estate instituted by God in the time of man's innocency signifying unto us the mystical union that is betwixt Christ and His Church.

Who isn't moved by these words?

Solemn vows are made at weddings. Couples commit themselves to each other "til *death* us do part'. They promise to love and uphold and care for each other. They promise to be faithful to each other, to have eyes only for each other, to esteem each other in the Lord.

> I take you to be my wedded wife, to have and to hold from this day forward, for better for worse, for richer for poorer, in sickness and in health, to love and to cherish — and she adds, to obey — 'til death us do part. According to God's holy ordinance and thereunto I plight thee my troth.

Sex

The bridegroom in this instance is an important figure — King Solomon, no less. In 3:11, he says, 'Go out, O daughters of Zion, and look upon King Solomon.' The women who have been addressed by the bride are now being urged by the bridegroom to take special notice of *him*.

But most of the attention is being given to the bride. As the young man begins to describe his bride, the language becomes extremely intimate. She is the centre of all of his attention. It is still the custom, even in the most liberated of circles, that the bride is the last to enter. She is the one that people talk about. It is this man she is going to marry. And now he has noticed her. In 4:1, he describes her as 'beautiful', and then in 4:7 as 'altogether beautiful'.

It is her wedding day. Hours and hours of preparation have gone into making her look as beautiful as it is possible to be on her wedding day. Have you ever seen a bride who doesn't look beautiful on her wedding day? She is wearing a veil, a 'diaphanous [delicate and translucent] muslin gauze', as one commentator somewhat unromantically describes it! It remains a part of the culture of wedding rituals to this day: the moment the vows are exchanged the veil is lifted, sometimes by the father as he hands her over to the bridegroom, and in some traditions the bridegroom himself does it. Sometimes, this is the first time the bridegroom has seen his bride!

Now the scene becomes very intimate. It looks as though we have moved from a public to a private setting, from the place of ceremony to the honeymoon suite. This is their wedding night, and he is telling her how beautiful she is. Smart man! It is interesting that as much as this passage is about sex and physical attraction, on another level it is also an appeal to her mind. It sounds as though he is quoting poetry to her on their wedding night!

It is all too common to think that sexual union is the most important aspect of marriage. But in saying this we need to be careful. As important as physical love is, there is *more* to marriage. Sex can be a purely physical thing. It is equally important that two people become one in mind as well as body. There is something quintessentially beautiful when two *minds* meet.

The Song of Solomon is about *words*, after all. It is about poetry. And the communication that is taking place here has meaning on several levels, not just the physical.

The Song of Solomon is not a complete book about love and marriage. This is a picture of two people on their wedding night, and what is said and what is happening here is entirely appropriate. But marriage is more than that. There isn't anything in the Song of Solomon about how you are supposed to respond when she has wrinkles, or when he has cancer, or when parts of your body do not work any more. What we have here is a picture of something that is as close to ideal as is possible in a fallen world.

In 4:1-7, she is smiling because he has just told her how beautiful she is. As she smiles, he notices that, well, her teeth are like 'a flock of shorn ewes' that have come up from the river, and not one of them is alone (v. 2). She has all her teeth! Forget about teeth whiteners, what's important here is that she has a full set!

He mentions other things; her lips and her neck are 'like the tower of David, and built in rows of stone' (v. 4). True, this does sound as though she ought to belong to an American football team, but think — *poetry*! Beauty is in the eye of the beholder, and as he continues his description, we weave our way through the similes and metaphors to what emerges as a description of their lovemaking. It all sounds exquisitely beautiful. But it is garden imagery. Enclosed, shut up, locked, and he alone has the key of entry. Read it. It is getting a little intimate now. He longs to be intimate with her and her with him.

Hedonistic obsession

Things have become a little hot! For this reason, there have been occasions when the Jews discouraged the reading of the Song of Solomon until you were thirty! In his book *Mere Christianity*, C. S. Lewis has a chapter called 'Sexual morality', where he writes:

> I'm sorry to have to go into all these details, but I must. The reason why I must is that you and I, for the last twenty years, have been fed all day long good, solid lies about sex. We've been told, until one is sick of hearing it, that sexual desire is in the same state as any of our other natural desires and that if only we abandon the silly old Victorian idea of hushing it up, everything in the garden would be lovely. It is not true.[2]

Wedding bells

There is something very powerful about sexual imagery, and it needs to be handled with a great deal of care. We are saturated with imagery of eroticism, particularly in the advertising world. Our current society has an insatiable need for sexual fulfilment. Television, Hollywood, literature, popular music — they're all *obsessed* with hedonistic sexuality.

I grew up in a different era, the days of *I Love Lucy* starring Desi Arnez and Lucille Ball. They slept in different beds on the TV show even though they were husband and wife! Do you remember that? It would have been inappropriate for them to have slept in the same bed on television. Whether that represented a distorted and somewhat prurient period is not the point. But our world is very different. That kind of 'innocence' (it wasn't, of course; it just appeared that way) has vanished. And in its wake has come a tidal wave of graphic sexuality. The internet has brought pornography into our very homes.

We can respond to all of this in several ways. We can surrender to our desires. We can do what the world says, 'Be a hedonist.' But we are Christians, and we cannot surrender to the world's agenda. We can deny these powerful forces. To a large extent, that is what the Roman Catholic Church did for centuries — imbibing a doctrine actually going back to Augustine and his doctrine of *concupiscence*. The term *concupiscence* refers in theology to the transmission of original sin and for Augustine this occurred from generation to generation through sexual intercourse. Augustine uses the term to include a form of instinctive sexual desire that was inseparable from normal human impulses. Sexual desire was bad because of its tendency to overwhelm. This is why the Catholic Church got into difficulties over birth control. They saw sexual union as only for the propagation of the race and no more. But that is to suggest that there is something evil within creation itself — a proto-Gnostic idea that has been around in one form or another from the very beginning of time.

Another possibility is to acknowledge that God has made us sexual beings, and has provided a forum in which this can be expressed in a loving, self-denying, Christ-glorifying way — *in marriage*. 'Therefore a man shall leave his father and his mother and hold fast to his wife, and they shall become one flesh. And the man and his wife were both naked and were not ashamed' (Genesis 2:24-25).

'Eudaimonism'[3]

The imagery of the second half of chapter four is about as graphic as you can find in Scripture, though it is still poetry. It is possible to read it and have no idea what it is saying. For the first time, he calls her his 'bride' (4:8).

Premarital sex is wrong; it is *always* wrong. It is wrong in every context, in every circumstance. It is just as much wrong for a man as it is for a woman. Sex is more than 'exchanging bodily fluids'. Sex before marriage is like moving into the house before you buy it. Once given away, it can never be retrieved. Never! However old-fashioned that may sound, Christians need to be clear about it. You have no business violating the virginity of another before you are married. You have no business doing that!

Here is some advice to girls: do not date a man who is dishonourable here. If he is prepared to violate your trust *before* you get married, what is to stop him *after* you get married? A few words in a church? It's a matter of commitment; it's a matter of *what* you are. Of course, girls can be equally promiscuous. And the point needs to be addressed to both sexes. That is why it is important to establish limits on physical courtship. Premarital sex isn't the unforgivable sin, and couples who have fallen here should be assured that there is a way forward, through confession of sin and repentance. But pre-marital sex should not be considered a trivial issue.

Wedding bells

I applaud young people who shamelessly assert that they are virgins until they get married. They wear T-shirts telling the whole world. I applaud them. I wouldn't have done it myself — wore the T-shirt, that is; but I applaud them! They are saying that they want to honour God in this. They are saying that they want their marriage to begin on the right footing.

Later in the Song of Solomon (chapter 8), there is a depiction of a young woman on the verge of puberty and sexual awareness. Her brothers come to her and say, in effect, 'You can be one of two things. You can be a wall, or you can be a door' (8:8-9). If she is a door, it means that anybody can enter. And if that is the case, these brothers are saying, they are going to have to build cedar walls around her.

In the church I serve, we ask very specific sexual-history questions of couples who want to get married. It is part of the policy of the church. They are asked to fill in a form and sign it. We make it clear that we think their partner deserves to know the answers before they get married! Better to find out before than afterwards! And often, the answers make for sad reading. Professing Christians have sexual histories that are often undistinguishable from the world in which we live.

Do you claim to be a follower of Jesus? Do you claim to have the Holy Spirit in your heart? You come to church, carry your Bible and read it, sing the hymns and claim to be a Christian. What does it mean to be a Christian? It should mean that I retain my virginity until I get married. That is what it *should* mean. I want God to have every part of me. I want God to have *this sexual* part of me. I want that first night of my wedding to be the most beautiful thing in the entire world. I want to be able to say on that night, 'I waited for you.' It means that I say to Jesus, 'I love you so much for what you have done for me. This is my response. I present my body a living sacrifice to you which is my reasonable act of worship.'

Will you do that? Will you make that promise? If you keep a diary, write something in it as a reminder: 'This is what I promise before God.' Tell your parents, if you can speak to your parents about these things.

Song of Solomon 5:2 - 6:3

SHE

2   *I slept, but my heart was awake.*
     A sound! My beloved is knocking.
     'Open to me, my sister, my love,
       my dove, my perfect one,
     for my head is wet with dew,
       my locks with the drops of the night.'

3   *I had put off my garment;*
       how could I put it on?
     I had bathed my feet;
       how could I soil them?

4   *My beloved put his hand to the latch,*
       and my heart was thrilled within me.

5   *I arose to open to my beloved,*
       and my hands dripped with myrrh,
     my fingers with liquid myrrh,
       on the handles of the bolt.

6   *I opened to my beloved,*
       but my beloved had turned and gone.
     My soul failed me when he spoke.

I sought him, but found him not;
   I called him, but he gave no answer.
7   *The watchmen found me*
      as they went about in the city;
   they beat me, they bruised me,
      they took away my veil,
      those watchmen of the walls.
8   *I adjure you, O daughters of Jerusalem,*
      if you find my beloved,
   that you tell him
      I am sick with love.

OTHERS

9   *What is your beloved more than another beloved,*
      O most beautiful among women?
   What is your beloved more than another beloved,
      that you thus adjure us?

SHE

10   *My beloved is radiant and ruddy,*
      distinguished among ten thousand.
11   *His head is the finest gold;*
      his locks are wavy,
      black as a raven.
12   *His eyes are like doves*
      beside streams of water,
   bathed in milk,
      sitting beside a full pool.
13   *His cheeks are like beds of spices,*
      mounds of sweet-smelling herbs.
   His lips are lilies,
      dripping liquid myrrh.
14   *His arms are rods of gold,*
      set with jewels.

His body is polished ivory,
bedecked with sapphires.
15 *His legs are alabaster columns,*
set on bases of gold.
His appearance is like Lebanon,
choice as the cedars.
16 *His mouth is most sweet,*
and he is altogether desirable.
This is my beloved and this is my friend,
O daughters of Jerusalem.

OTHERS

6 *Where has your beloved gone,*
O most beautiful among women?
Where has your beloved turned,
that we may seek him with you?

SHE

2 *My beloved has gone down to his garden*
to the beds of spices,
to graze in the gardens
and to gather lilies.
3 *I am my beloved's and my beloved is mine;*
he grazes among the lilies.

5.

Love in winter

Suddenly, after the quarrel, while we waited,
  Disheartened, silent, with downcast looks, nor stirred
Eyelid nor finger, hopeless both, yet hoping
  Against all hope to unsay the sundering word:

While all the room's stillness deepened, deepened about us
  And each of us crept his thought's way to discover
How, with as little sound as the fall of a leaf,
  The shadow had fallen, and lover quarrelled with lover.

CONRAD AIKEN [1889–1973]

And they lived happily ever after. Isn't that the way it is supposed to end? That's how fairy tales end, but life in a fallen world never ends that way. The dream of the wedding day gives way to reality.

Problems now seem to arise in our couple's relationship. We shouldn't press the historical sequence too far, suggesting that this occurs immediately after their wedding! In the best of stories, we could simply interject 'Some time later' at this point. This is not so much the next day, but the next scene. We've turned the page and this is 'Mr and Mrs Beautiful' sometime later.

'Realism' is the word that comes to mind. The bliss of marriage has turned to the humdrum of surviving those difficult days when something has happened to upset the equilibrium. A sense of unfairness has arisen. Or maybe it is the sheer routine of their existence. The spark has gone and they are conscious, not so much of what drew them together, but what keeps them apart.

We live in an age, in a world, in a church, in which a measure of realism is necessary. It may well have seemed different when some of us were growing up, and it probably was. But those are not the days we live in, and we need to turn to this book that God has given to us, and that the Holy Spirit has inspired. In the very centre of our Bibles, God says that there is something pure and there is something beautiful about a man and a woman who are married and who are engaging in the most intimate of relations together. There is something astonishingly beautiful about it.

The scene opens with what appears to be the young woman half-asleep, and someone is knocking at the door! There are some delicacies here. Remember that these are pictures of a normal married couple!

> 2   *I slept, but my heart was awake.*
> *A sound! My beloved is knocking.*
> *'Open to me, my sister, my love,*
>   *my dove, my perfect one,*
> *for my head is wet with dew,*
>   *my locks with the drops of the night.'*
>
> 3   *I had put off my garment;*
>   *how could I put it on?*
> *I had bathed my feet;*
>   *how could I soil them?*

4   *My beloved put his hand to the latch,*
       and my heart was thrilled within me.
5   *I arose to open to my beloved,*
       and my hands dripped with myrrh,
    my fingers with liquid myrrh,
       on the handles of the bolt.
6   *I opened to my beloved,*
       but my beloved had turned and gone.
    My soul failed me when he spoke.
    I sought him, but found him not;
       I called him, but he gave no answer.

She wakes in the morning to find that he has gone. Something is wrong. We are not quite sure at first what it is, but there is tension in the air. Perhaps one of those marital tiffs has surfaced again: he is knocking at the door, and she is playing hard to get!

Then she changes her mind and opens the door. And he is not there anymore. He's gone. In a huff, perhaps! Before the end of this section, they will be together again. But for now, she is distraught and looking for him.

Is this a dream? Is this just poetry? Is this describing something as historically vivid as what we've just described? It's hard to know. One thing is for certain: this couple is experiencing marital difficulty.

Marriages experience strife

It all begins with a husband knocking on the door (5:2). Let's imagine a scene…

He has been at work, and now he is knocking on the door. It is meant to be a rerun of chapter 4, but things are not going his way. Here is the picture. It is night time; she has gone to bed. She is tired of waiting for her husband to come home. He has been at the office; he is working. There is a big case tomorrow. He has a file, a report, to prepare.

It is really late. Actually, he may even have been with his sheep — he's a farmer, you understand. Whatever he was doing, he finally finishes his task. Was he simply trying to teach her a lesson by staying away for a while?

He has been drinking coffee by the gallon and he is wide awake, and he's driving home. He has conjugal rights on his mind. He jumps out of his car, puts the key into the door and it is bolted — *from the inside*!

He suddenly notices it is morning already. The dew has descended and his hair is wet. And he cannot get into his own house.

'Darling! I'm home!' he's shouting, knocking on the door.

'Let me in…'

It is more than possible that the poetry is meant to be far more suggestive, far more intimate. But let's just go with this picture for a moment. He cannot get in. 'I'll use sweet talk,' he thinks. That should do it; a little poetry — with Nora Jones playing in the background.

'My sister, my love, my dove, my perfect one.'

Well, isn't he the romantic? But she is seriously miffed. Her feelings have been hurt. He should have been home hours ago. He never called. The dinner's in the dog, and she's playing a familiar tune, 'I'll show him who's in charge here.'

'I had put off my garment; how could I put it on?' she says (5:3). It is winter, perhaps. It is cold; the door was far away. She needed to put something on.

'I had bathed my feet; how could I soil them?' Well, in effect, she is saying, 'I've got a headache!'

He's going to have to stay outside with the dog, who is sound asleep after having eaten his dinner. There is a sign above the door now, and it says, 'Turbulence ahead'. (Isn't this a delightful scene? It almost sounds like a TV soap opera, except this is in the Bible!)

Now he's got his hand through the wooden door. Imagine an old-fashioned lock — a wooden lever that goes up and down so that you have to put your hand in to push the lever. Just think along those lines for a minute.

He's trying to get in, and he's saying, 'Darling, let me in.' But she is still 'stewing'. And she's saying to herself, 'I need to wait a few minutes because he needs to be taught a lesson.'

Then she relents. She gets up, opens the door, and she says, 'I'm sorry!' But he's not there; he has gone! You can just imagine the scene as she stares at the empty porch. *He has gone! How could he have gone?*

You see, two can play at that game. It's called, 'Let's see who can sulk the most.' He has been tender. Well, he has been a cad, too, for not coming home, but he has also been tender. She, on the other hand, has been stewing — maybe for hours, and she's determined to give this rehearsed speech.

She gets dressed; she starts looking for him. She goes out into the night. She is wandering around the streets, and well, she's set upon. She's assaulted; and part of her clothing is torn away from her. Things have gone from bad to worse.

Perhaps this is all just a bad dream. (There are shades of 1 Corinthians 7:3 here: 'The husband should give to his wife her conjugal rights, and likewise the wife to her husband.') Her feelings are seriously hurt. He never imagined that he was doing anything bad — certainly not as bad as she was making out.

He thinks: 'I'm working all the hours there are to provide her with what she needs. You know, the SUV, the lunches with her friends, the membership in the Tennis Club, the beach house, and this is what I get. It's so unfair. She ought to be grateful, but no, she always wants more. She is never satisfied. She ought to have the dinner waiting for me when I get home and be grateful when I come! That's what!'

She thinks: 'I need to teach him who's the boss around here. All I'm asking is that he come home at a reasonable time. All I'm asking is that he come home and sit down for dinner like my mum and dad used to do. He's thoughtless; he's a brute. I have every right to be angry.'

Anger management

Marriages experience strife. Yes, the most glamorous of them experience strife. They begin with things like selfishness, and inconsideration, and greed, and the 'me-ism' that marks so much of our existence.

Men are from Mars, and women are from Venus; they're different. So, who is to blame here? The one who causes the hurt feelings or the one who takes them?

Me, me, me. I love myself.
I have a picture on my shelf.

We are into a section on the management of anger. Do you see what is happening here? A lack of *kenosis*. *Kenosis* is what Paul says Christ did in the incarnation. 'Who, though he was in the form of God, did not count equality with God a thing to be grasped, but made himself nothing [lit. "emptied himself"]' (Philippians 2:5-7). Jesus made himself nothing. He didn't insist upon his rights. He didn't stand upon his dignity. He didn't always *insist* upon his entitlements, but for the sake of our salvation, he denied himself. He became *a servant*. And Paul adds, 'Let this mind be in you, which was also in Christ Jesus' (Philippians 2:5, AV).

Self-denial is what is called for in marriage as much as in any part of our lives. Both lacked self-denial in this tale of early married life. How does that work in marriage? It means that when you love someone, you don't always stand on your dignity. You don't always insist upon your rights. You deny yourself for the sake of the one you love. That is what Jesus did for us; that is what the cross is all about.

'Whoever is slow to anger is better than the mighty, and he who rules his spirit than he who takes a city' (Proverbs 16:32).

'Better is a dry morsel with quiet than a house full of feasting with strife' (17:1).

'The north wind brings forth rain, and a backbiting tongue, angry looks. It is better to live in a corner of the housetop than in a house shared with a quarrelsome wife' (25:23-24).

'For lack of wood the fire goes out, and where there is no whisperer, quarrelling ceases. As charcoal to hot embers and wood to fire, so is a quarrelsome man for kindling strife' (26:20-21).

Something relatively minor has escalated now into something really major. The desire for revenge, to 'get even' in the marriage, has got both of them into trouble. He has put her in a place of vulnerability by his stupidity.

Friends *and* lovers

In the second section (5:10 – 6:3), she is recalling why she married this man in the first place. It is all a little over the top, as romantic thoughts can be. He is more handsome than ten thousand men (5:10). She talks about his head, his pale skin, his red cheeks, his black hair; his eyes are like doves (vv. 11-12). The white of his eyes can be seen. I think she means he is clean living — there's no evidence of alcohol abuse.

She mentions his lips: his words are like dripping myrrh (v. 13). His body (v. 14), his legs (v. 15) — the description is flamboyant. Middle-aged spread hasn't reshaped this young man yet!

But there's one word that deserves special attention. She says at the very end of this description, he is 'my friend' (5:16). We should take note of that. At the end of this description of her husband, she wants him again. She cannot find him and she is sorry. She is describing him in this over-the-top poetic way; but in the end, she misses him because he is her best friend.

Marriage is about friendship. Do you recall Genesis 2: the passage where Adam is naming all the animals? It is about companionship. Adam names the animals: the four-legged hairy creature which he calls 'dog'. And here comes this swanky thing, and it's a 'cat'. This odd, clucking creature is 'chicken'. True, Adam didn't speak English and so didn't name them 'dog', or 'cat', or 'chicken', but the point of the passage is about companionship. Of all the creatures God made, none was a true companion for Adam. You can have a relationship with a dog. I love my dog! But, at the end of the day he doesn't like Wagner. He leaves the room when I put Wagner on my CD player — every time!

It is true that in this fallen world there are people who have been so hurt by fellow human beings that they find they can be closer to animals than they can be to human beings. I fully understand that.

Yet if we turn back to Genesis 2, there is that wonderful moment when God takes a rib out of Adam's side and makes a woman, as a 'helpmeet' for him — a companion, a friend, a soul mate. 'And the rib that the LORD God had taken from the man he made into a woman and brought her to the man. Then the man said, "This at last is bone of my bones and flesh of my flesh; she shall be called Woman, because she was taken out of Man." Therefore a man shall leave his father and his mother and hold fast to his wife, and they shall become one flesh. And the man and his wife were both naked and were not ashamed' (Genesis 2:22-25).

This passage in the Song of Solomon is all about physical intimacy and sexuality; but it is also about friendship. The linchpin of a lasting marriage is friendship; couples who have a mutual respect for, and enjoyment of, each other's company. You know exactly how they're going to respond. You know what every little gesture means. You like being in their presence; you like their company; you like their personality; you like the odd things, the quirky things about them. You share in their dreams.

Friends forgive each other's failures. Friends miss each other when parted. They love to talk to each other. They say things like, 'I like the things you like. I like it when you put up with the things you don't like because I like them.' Too many married couples treat their spouses one way and their friends another way. If you treated your friends like you treat your spouse, would you have any friends? What tone of voice do you most often use with your spouse? She says, 'He's my friend.'

• Friends accept each other as they are. That doesn't mean that you don't aspire them to be something better and greater. Some folk need projects. They aren't happy unless they've got something to fix. They bring home stray animals. They adopt needy people. They get into marriages on the same premise. I understand that, but friends accept the way you are.

- Friends like to spend time with each other — solitary time. You can tell if you are a friend if you like to be together and actually say nothing, even for long periods. By this, I do not mean those long periods when you have just had an argument and are sulking or not speaking to each other. No, I do not mean that.

- Friends have a deep affection for one another. Affection is more than sex. It's romance, smiles and good manners. It's 'please' and 'thank you'. Affection makes requests rather than bark orders. Married friends are kind to each other. You can give that little knowing wink — that gesture in the middle of a crowd — in the middle of another person's conversation, and you know exactly what your spouse is thinking.

- Friends laugh a lot. There is a side to my wife that most don't know, but there are certain things that can make her completely lose it. The giggles! They may take fifteen minutes to get over, and once they start, there's no stopping them. It's friendship.

- Friends trust each other. They trust each other with their deepest secrets. They trust each other with their failures. They trust each other with their sins. Friends are trusted confidants. Friends look out for each other and take sides together against the world.

Happy endings

The poem ends a little strangely. It seems that she knew where he was all along! 'Typical!' you might be tempted to say. But there's double meaning here. The scene has changed and they are together. 'My beloved has gone down to his garden to the beds of spices, to graze in the gardens and to gather lilies. I am my beloved's and my beloved is mine; he grazes among the lilies' (6:2-3).

I do not need to spell this out to you; I am sure you have guessed it. They have kissed and made up. They have found each other; they are embracing again. In the old movies, this is the point at which the camera veers away from the couple, focuses on the wallpaper and the couple fade out of the picture as the music rises to 'The End' and the credits roll.

They kiss and make up.

And it is none of our business what goes on after this!

Song of Solomon 6:4 - 8:4

H<small>E</small>

4   *You are beautiful as Tirzah, my love,*
      lovely as Jerusalem,
      awesome as an army with banners.

5   *Turn away your eyes from me,*
      for they overwhelm me —
   Your hair is like a flock of goats
      leaping down the slopes of Gilead.

6   *Your teeth are like a flock of ewes*
      that have come up from the washing;
   all of them bear twins;
      not one among them has lost its young.

7   *Your cheeks are like halves of a pomegranate*
      behind your veil.

8   *There are sixty queens and eighty concubines,*
      and virgins without number.

9   *My dove, my perfect one, is the only one,*
      the only one of her mother,
      pure to her who bore her.
   The young women saw her and called her blessed;
      the queens and concubines also, and they praised
      her.

10   *'Who is this who looks down like the dawn,*
        beautiful as the moon, bright as the sun,
        awesome as an army with banners?'

SHE

11   *I went down to the nut orchard*
        to look at the blossoms of the valley,
   to see whether the vines had budded,
        whether the pomegranates were in bloom.
12   *Before I was aware, my desire set me*
        among the chariots of my kinsman, a prince.

OTHERS

13   *Return, return, O Shulammite,*
        return, return, that we may look upon you.

HE

Why should you look upon the Shulammite,
        as upon a dance before two armies?

7   *How beautiful are your feet in sandals,*
        O noble daughter!
   Your rounded thighs are like jewels,
        the work of a master hand.
2   *Your navel is a rounded bowl*
        that never lacks mixed wine.
   Your belly is a heap of wheat,
        encircled with lilies.
3   *Your two breasts are like two fawns,*
        twins of a gazelle.
4   *Your neck is like an ivory tower.*
   Your eyes are pools in Heshbon,
        by the gate of Bath-rabbim.
   Your nose is like a tower of Lebanon,

which looks towards Damascus.
5   *Your head crowns you like Carmel,*
        and your flowing locks are like purple;
        a king is held captive in the tresses.

6   *How beautiful and pleasant you are,*
        O loved one, with all your delights!
7   *Your stature is like a palm tree,*
        and your breasts are like its clusters.
8   *I say I will climb the palm tree*
        and lay hold of its fruit.
    Oh may your breasts be like clusters of the vine,
        and the scent of your breath like apples,
9   *and your mouth like the best wine.*

SHE
It goes down smoothly for my beloved,
    gliding over lips and teeth.
10   *I am my beloved's,*
        and his desire is for me.

11   *Come, my beloved,*
        let us go out into the fields
        and lodge in the villages;
12   *let us go out early to the vineyards*
        and see whether the vines have budded,
    whether the grape blossoms have opened
        and the pomegranates are in bloom.
    There I will give you my love.
13   *The mandrakes give forth fragrance,*
        and beside our doors are all choice fruits,
    new as well as old,
        which I have laid up for you,
            O my beloved.

8 *Oh that you were like a brother to me*
who nursed at my mother's breasts!
If I found you outside, I would kiss you,
and none would despise me.
2 *I would lead you and bring you*
into the house of my mother —
she who used to teach me.
I would give you spiced wine to drink,
the juice of my pomegranate.
3 *His left hand is under my head,*
and his right hand embraces me!
4 *I adjure you, O daughters of Jerusalem,*
that you not stir up or awaken love
until it pleases.

6.

Communicating affection

If ever two were one then surely we.
　　If ever man were loved by wife, then thee;
If ever wife were happy in a man,
　　Compare with me, ye women, if you can.
I prize thy love more than whole mines of gold
　　Or all the riches that the East doth hold.
My love is such that rivers cannot quench,
　　Nor aught but love from thee give recompense.
Thy love is such I can no way repay,
　　The heavens reward thee manifold, I pray.
Then while we live, in love let's so persevere
　　That when we live no more, we may live ever.

ANNE BRADSTREET (1612-72)

It is hot in chapter 7 of the Song of Solomon. The little tiff that marked much of the last section is over. It is back to sweet talk, *really* sweet talk, mainly by the man about his bride. At least one major commentator believes that the squabble in chapter 5 actually took place *during* the wedding festivities! In the Middle East these festivities would go on for days, and we are now only a few days after the wedding that is described in chapters 3 and 4. Even so, this is poetry, and it is possible to overdo the underlying storyline.

However, this may be many months after the wedding. There has been a quarrel, a misunderstanding, a tiff, and she had bolted the door, you will remember. When he came home, he could not get in. Then, as chapter 6:1-3 closed, we left the two alone. Now it is time to join them again. We are going to listen to what they are saying to each other. After a quarrel, there has to be some talking. The air has to be cleared. Misunderstandings have to be rectified. Words have to be spoken.

The sting of words spoken in haste and bitterness sometimes takes a long time to heal. It takes work. It takes effort to heal that damage, and what we see here in chapters 6 and 7 are words of affection. In this case, it is particularly the man who communicates affection.

He is doing all that sweet talk again. Some of what he says about her hair, teeth, neck and so on is repetition of what we have heard before in chapter 4, on his wedding night — her hair like a flock of goats, her teeth like a flock of sheep (6:5). It probably would not work for most of us nowadays, but it evidently sounded wonderful in the tenth century B.C.

However, there are differences now. He omits certain things that he had mentioned on his wedding night. He doesn't mention now her lips or her breasts or her hips, at least not initially, because he wants her to understand that she is more important to him than merely gratifying some physical pleasure. The suspicion that there's only one thing on this man's mind needs to be overcome, for he speaks to her in such endearing terms. There are more important things in a relationship than sexual gratification. He wants his motives to be purer than that. It's time to speak.

He could have gone off with wounded pride, he could have sulked, he could have gone to his office and put his telephone on 'do not disturb'. He could have told his secretary to say, 'He's in a meeting.' He could have given her the silent treatment. 'I'll teach her to be grateful,' he could have said. He could have become psychologically abusive. He wouldn't have been the first to do so. He could have thrown his weight around; he could have shown her the 'man' that he was. He could have insisted on his rights, and he could have told her that she was nothing without him.

I heard a young woman tearfully say to me once that her husband had said to her, 'No one wants used goods.' The husband in the Song could have said that! He could have beaten her up, forcing her to camouflage the bruises, stay at home and make excuses so that she would not have to appear in public and give all kinds of embarrassing explanations. Things could have gone very sour. This woman could have found herself in the beginnings of an abusive relationship that could have gone on for years and would have ended up, perhaps, with her having to leave him for her own safety, or for the safety of her children.

He could have justified to himself an affair. This is how they begin. He could have begun to see his wife as a live-in maid, who cooks and cleans for him, and looks pretty when he invites his friends over. He could have done that, and found his satisfaction elsewhere. Instead, these two engage in the language of reconciliation. The man takes his responsibility; he initiates communication of affection for her.

They say flattery will get you nowhere, but sometimes we just do not know how to take a compliment. Marital reconciliation begins on this note. Let's listen to them for a minute. Let's eavesdrop on the very sensitive personal communication between these two.

Talk

He begins and ends, in verses 4 and 10 of chapter 6, by saying how beautiful she is. That is how he starts. Isn't that something to note? I think it is. The first words out of his mouth are, 'How beautiful you are.' That's right. You may be suspecting his motives. You may be saying, 'Words are cheap.' Actually, in my experience, for men words are about the most expensive things you can get, especially in situations like this. A harsh word stirs up anger, Solomon says.

It is time for softly spoken words, affirming words, reconciling words, endearing words. Let's imagine how this *could* have started:

'Let me tell you, *dear*, where you went wrong!'
'You're just like your mother!'
'John's wife *never* behaves like this!'
'I'm giving you one more chance to say you're sorry!'

Yet he never mentions what she did; he never brings it up. Instead of picking on the dead carcass of bitterness like a vulture, he lets it go. Clara Barton, founder of the Red Cross in the United States, was asked in an interview about a bad incident in her past, and she said, 'I distinctly remember forgetting that.' Isn't that good? 'I distinctly remember forgetting that.'

'Have this mind among yourselves, which is yours in Christ Jesus' (Philippians 2:5).
'Husbands, love your wives, as Christ loved the church and gave himself up for her' (Ephesians 5:25).
'Sweetness of speech increases persuasiveness' (Proverbs 16:21).
'Gracious words are like a honeycomb, sweetness to the soul and health to the body' (Proverbs 16:24).

Did you notice how he does not allow himself to get distracted from what he needs to say to her? He says in verse 5, 'Turn away your eyes from me, for they overwhelm me.' 'Don't look at me because I just won't be able to say what I need to say. I need to say these things to you. So turn your eyes away for a second.' That's what he's saying. His heart is ablaze for this woman. This is the hardest part, isn't it? Affirming your spouse's qualities; getting off your high horse of wounded pride and ending the 'pity party'.

He reminds himself in verse 9 of why he married this woman. 'My dove, my perfect one, is the only one.' 'You are the only one,' he says. To him, she is more important than anything else in the world. She has no equal. He has eyes only for her. That's a challenge, isn't it? It shouldn't be, but when you are wounded, that can become a challenge. You treat your husband badly and sometimes push him away, and he becomes vulnerable.

Then all sorts of things can happen. He starts talking to his secretary. It is all innocent enough, to begin with. At least, it seems that way. She listens and is sympathetic. He finds himself saying, 'She understands me.' He conveniently forgets that she's paid to 'understand' him! What appears so very innocent is laden with danger.

Lost in translation

This first part of the poem in chapter 6 ends with the couple going off to the nut orchard (v. 11); specifically, walnuts, and she is looking for signs of spring. Suddenly, they find themselves transported onto a chariot, and the two of them are riding away. Right! There are deeper allusions and double meanings here, too.

Chapter 7 begins with this intimate, in fact, *extremely* intimate, conversation between the man and this bride of his. There are things in chapter 7 that you definitely need to be over 30 to understand! It is a love poem of the most intense nature. He is describing her, this time beginning at the feet and working upward. In previous poems, he started from the head and worked down, but this time he is starting from the feet and works upwards. Commentators vie with each other to see who is the most daring as to what they see in these allusions.

There is poetic licence here. She does not really have purple hair. Nor has she forgotten her 'Lifesavers' because her breath smells of wine — or is it apple cider? Nor is he thinking of Steve Martin in *Roxanne*, when he describes her nose as 'the tower of Lebanon'. Contextualization means we should not try this at home! It is rather like listening to Italian opera in English — the words can sometimes sound a little banal. But there are a few things to note.

First, imagine the two of them having been reconciled, and now going off in this chariot together to talk, etc. Marriage shouldn't end dating. Is this stretching the point, exegetically? I don't think so. They are going off together because they need to talk to each other. I love that. There is an elder in the congregation where I minister who asked me about seven years ago, 'When did you last date your wife?' 'Americans!' is what I thought! I was trying to finish a Ph.D. I was trying to write twelve new courses to teach at the seminary. In addition, I was preaching every Sunday. I had made some very poor judgement calls.

I have never forgotten that question. And I have tried hard to make amends, because keeping romance alive can be a real challenge when you are juggling a lot of duties.

Inspiring fresh feelings for one another takes commitment and creativity. You need to separate work life from private life. My mother said to me on my wedding day, on the steps of the church, 'Remember,' she said, 'when the children are gone, she's the only one you've got.' I'm certain it was something much more eloquent than that, but that is what I remember. I had just been married a few minutes before! 'I don't have any children,' I protested. But I knew what she meant. It is all too easy to divert our attention on our children and find we have forgotten how to love the one we married.

Second, notice also the language of maturity here. Love ought to grow. There is a greater maturity; there is even a greater intensity to what he says in chapter 7, compared to what he described in chapter 4, on his wedding night. The details are greater; he is a little more experienced now. You know the jokes. 'Marriage is a great institution, but who wants to live in an institution?' 'Man is incomplete until he is married, and then he is finished.' 'Marriage is not a word it is a sentence, a life sentence.' You have heard them all. What I think we see here, in a small way, is the growing love that he has for his bride.

As I was looking at this chapter, I was trying to find a word to sum it up; and realized that there is a tenderness to chapter 7. The man is so tender. His words are so tender. If he isn't, what will happen? I'll tell you what will happen. She will look for appreciation somewhere else. Maybe she'll start working and spend more time out of the house. Maybe she'll visit her mother more often. Maybe she'll spend time with her friends. Maybe she'll devote all of her attention to the children. One day she'll find herself in a café somewhere, and she'll hear a voice, a man's voice, saying to her, 'Do you come in here often?' And she says, 'I come in here every Tuesday.' Now, she never goes on Tuesday, but for some reason she wanted him to know she'd be there next Tuesday. It has begun. It has started. I'm saying to us men, we need to learn the language of this tenderness. This book is inspired by the Holy Spirit and is here for a reason.

Time to go

What we have described here took place in public view. There has been some sort of party; there seems to be dancing at the end of chapter 6, but by the time we get to 7:11, the bride says to her husband, 'It's time to go home.' 'Come, my beloved, let us go out into the fields and lodge in the villages.' When she starts talking about mandrakes and pomegranates, we have moved into the most intimate of situations. When we come to 8:3, 'his left hand is under my head and his right hand embraces me', we all understand what she is saying. But what is interesting is that there is a time and place for everything. What we have here belongs, as she seems to indicate in 7:11, at another location.

Did you notice at the beginning of chapter 8 she says, 'Oh that you were like a brother to me'? That is a little strange, isn't it? You know, they are having this wonderful sweet talk and he is doing his level best to speak this effusive language of tenderness, affection and poetry, and she responds by saying, 'I wish you were my brother.' She is not saying, 'Let's just be friends.' In the culture in which she found herself, public displays of affection would have been frowned upon. She could not even have kissed him in public — her brother, yes, but not her husband. Now, we may find that difficult to understand. It is not the society in which we live. We are a million miles away from this culture. Yet I have to tell you, husbands, that in Belfast, Northern Ireland, if you put your arm around your wife in a church, in a public worship service, it is considered wholly inappropriate. In fact, it is frowned upon. They would say, 'Americans! Too much display of public affection.' What we have here is just a little snippet, an insight into how cultures change and affect even the display of certain things. Paul says in the New Testament, 'Greet one another with a holy kiss' (2 Corinthians 13:12). We do not do that in the UK or USA. We shake hands, maybe hug, but no more than that. We would rarely greet one another with a holy kiss. There are cultural expressions, and this is one of them.

These two are going off to be alone now. What they do is none of our business. But notice what she says to the women before she goes: 'I adjure you, O daughters of Jerusalem, that you not stir up or awaken love until it pleases' (8:4). Things are getting hot here, and she gives a warning to the women, her friends, perhaps. She has said it twice before (cf. 2:7; 3:5), and now repeats it again. There are things here, sexual drive, and stimulation, and affection, that are so powerful that you dare not stir them up if you are not in a position to consummate them. These daughters of Jerusalem were more than likely unmarried women. She is telling them that they need to be careful.

A young man who had gone off to college once said to me, 'That's my prayer, that I will remain a virgin until I get married.'

Then I scribbled something in the back of his Bible.

I said to him, 'When you're tempted, call me and we'll talk it through,' and wrote out my phone number.

Song of Solomon 8:5-7 [1]

OTHERS

5 *Who is that coming up from the wilderness,*
  leaning on her beloved?

SHE

Under the apple tree I awakened you.
There your mother was in labour with you;
 there she who bore you was in labour.

6 *Set me as a seal upon your heart,*
  as a seal upon your arm,
for love is strong as death,
 jealousy is fierce as the grave.
Its flashes are flashes of fire,
 the very flame of the LORD.

7 *Many waters cannot quench love,*
 neither can floods drown it.
If a man offered for love
 all the wealth of his house,
 he would be utterly despised.

7.

Love's commitments

O lift me from the grass!
　I die! I faint! I fail!
Let thy love in kisses rain
　On my lips and eyelids pale.
My cheek is cold and white, alas!
　My heart beats loud and fast; —
Oh! Press it to thine own again,
　Where it will break at last.

PERCY BYSSHE SHELLEY (1792–1822)

Wilt thou have this man to thy wedded husband, to live together after God's ordinance in the holy estate of matrimony? Wilt thou obey him, and serve him, love, honour, and keep him in sickness and in health; and, forsaking all other, keep thee only unto him, so long as ye both shall live?

These, of course, are the words of Thomas Cranmer in the *Book of Common Prayer*, first published in 1545. It urges the bride to 'keep thee only unto him'. And, of course, there is a similar one, 'keep thee only unto her'. The final poem in the Song (8:5-14) is a meditation on the power of love, and in this chapter we will consider only the opening section in which the young woman[2] is recalling how, *underneath an apple tree* (cf. 2:3, 5; 7:8), she had awakened his love. Maybe she is thinking of the place where they did some of their courting. More likely, she is recalling the location where their union first found expression — the honeymoon suite!

She has thoughts about his mother. No, not the 'mother-in-law' kind! She is either recalling that they spent their honeymoon in his mother's bed (a very probable scenario), or she is expressing the idea that his mother bore him for her. The poetry is a little difficult to understand, but she's making a statement about destiny: 'There your mother was in labour with you; there she who bore you was in labour' (v. 5). It is the thought that she had given birth to the one who would be her husband, and that there was a destiny, or more properly, a *providence* to it. God was in this. God had planned this. This isn't just some coincidence. This is ordered of the Lord. This is how it should be. This is how it has turned out, according to a plan, a purpose, because there is wisdom behind it.

Painted periwinkles!

She is thinking about her husband's love for her, how precious it is and how focused it is — on her, and not anyone else. 'Set me as a seal upon your heart, as a seal upon your arm, for love is strong as death' (8:6).

Marriage is like a seal, a signature of authenticity, of ownership. If you are going to purchase what 'Mrs Bouquet' of the UK's television programme *Keeping Up Appearances* calls 'a piece of Royal Doulton china, complete with hand-painted periwinkles', you had better make sure there is a seal underneath the cup, or plate, or saucer. It is the sign of authenticity, signifying that it is the genuine article. Paul refers to the Holy Spirit as God's seal (cf. Ephesians 1:13-14), God's mark of authentication, signifying that a genuine work of change and renewal has taken place in our lives.

Now, she is saying several things here. And, yes, it is in the form of a request, but I think we can safely say that this is what she thinks marriage is. She speaks, first of all, about the seal of the heart. She wants him to place her as a seal upon his heart. She wants to be loved by him: she wants his affection, and she wants all that that affection entails.

It is often quoted, especially at weddings, and it is often attributed to Matthew Henry, but it was Peter Lombard in the Medieval period who first coined the words, that Eve was formed from the rib of Adam, 'not out of his head to rule over him, not from his foot to be trampled under him, but out of his side, to be cared for by him, near to his heart to be loved by him, under his arm to be protected by him'.[3] She wants to be loved by him. She wants the loyalty of his heart and his affections. That is what she is saying.

It is one of those moments that arise from time to time. They are unpredictable occasions, but they come along, and she asks, 'Do you love me?' These are definitive moments. And husbands know that 'pat' answers will not suffice. If they do not know it, trouble is sure to ensue. She is saying, 'I want you to put me as the seal on your heart.' She did not want to be married to a man with a wandering eye, but to someone who only has eyes for her, who is in love with her, and is prepared to say so. Often!

Men struggle with lust. Some men fall prey to it a great deal. Job was one of the holiest men in the ancient near east, and yet even Job says that he made a covenant with his eyes not to look lustfully after a girl (cf. Job 31:1). The apostle John talks about the lust of the eyes (cf. 1 John 2:16, AV). Origen, in the third century, was so offended by this in his life that — and there is no delicate way I can possibly put this — he emasculated himself using two bricks! Jonathan Edwards complained about the prevalence of inordinate lust in eighteenth-century Puritan New England.[4]

This is the place, I think, to talk about pornography. Forgive me, but we do need to deal with it. There is no place for pornography, anywhere, anytime, for any purpose. Leviticus 18 makes this absolutely crystal clear: to look on the naked body of someone who is not your spouse is more than lust; it is adultery. Nothing is more demeaning to a woman, or for that matter to a man, than pornography. Nothing is more crippling to you in your relationship with your wife. 'Do you love me?' she is saying. I want you to place me as the seal on your heart. I want your undivided affection.

Today, she might express that concern in different ways. Husbands who misuse the Internet, or who engage in chat-room fantasy, cross significant boundaries. Sexual fulfilment is found in a loving relationship between a husband and a wife. It isn't meant to be between you and a picture or movie. It isn't meant to be with you and a virtual mate on a computer. Lust is never satisfied. It always craves for more. Its power is intense and addictive. 'But among you there must not be even a hint of sexual immorality' (Ephesians 5:3, NIV).

Did you notice what she says here about jealousy?

...love is strong as death,
    jealousy is fierce as the grave.
Its flashes are flashes of fire,
    the very flame of the LORD (v. 6).

Jealousy! Is there a place for *jealousy* in a relationship between a husband and a wife? Surely, jealousy is a bad thing. We speak of a jealous wife or a jealous husband in a pejorative sense. In the sixteen things that Paul lists as the works of the flesh, one of them is jealousy (cf. Galatians 5:20).

Gustav Mahler (1860-1911), perhaps one of the greatest composers who has ever lived, was insanely jealous of his wife's abilities. When he married Alma Shindler, she too was a composer in her own right. But he couldn't cope with the applause and plaudits she was getting. So he wrote a note to her on the day of their wedding. 'From now on,' he said, 'there will only be my music. Not our music but my music.'[5] As all the biographers seem to point out, it was an occasion of incredible jealousy. The marriage was rocky and didn't last.

Yet jealousy *can* express itself in both righteous and unrighteous ways. God is described in the Bible as a jealous God! In Exodus 34, God says his name is 'jealous' (cf. Exodus 24:6). When it comes to the worship of Egyptian deities, in the context of which Moses is writing the book of Exodus, God is utterly intolerant. He will not share worship with another. He is jealous for his own name. And a spouse is equally intolerant of the inappropriate affections given to someone else rather than to her. If the spouse is signalling their dreams and aspirations to someone of the opposite sex, there may well be reasons for appropriate jealousy. If you eat alone with someone else of the opposite sex, you are skirting danger. Marriage was meant for two, and only two. 'I want you to place me as a seal on your heart,' she says. And she has every right to ask that.

Tattoos!

She also asks to be placed as a seal *on his arm*. That's a little more difficult. Tattoos come to mind. You know the ones: a heart with 'Jane' written on it! It is more likely that she is saying, 'I want you to be my protector. I want you to take charge. I want you to take ownership of this marriage.' Let's pursue that.

The Bible teaches that husbands and wives have complementary roles to play in marriage. In our sexually confused age, there is uncertainty as to what gender is, let alone the roles that genders are meant to play. For example, Smith College, the historic women's institution, has amended its student constitution to exclude the pronouns 'she' and 'her'. Why? As a news story explained, 'A growing number of students identify themselves as transgender, and say they feel uncomfortable with female pronouns.'[6]

By employing Christ's relationship to the church as a model of what marriage ought to be, Paul highlights the husband's special responsibility as leader and protector, and the wife's calling to accept her husband in that role (Ephesians 5:21-33). Men and women are equally God's image-bearers (Genesis 1:27), and as a result share equal dignity. Their genders complement each other as each finds expression in marriage, procreation and family life (Genesis 2:18-23). Learning these differences and appreciating them as created by God is the way to both happiness and spiritual growth. Only as husbands and wives rest in and show respect for the mystery of their differences can true satisfaction be found. *Vive la difference!*

There is, sadly, an inappropriate way to express leadership in a marriage. What is meant to be loving and protective can turn into domination and bullying in a fallen world. But distortions do not and should not negate the principle. Abuse should lead us to demonstrate the benefits of living the way God intends men and women to live.

It is as though the young woman in our poem is saying, 'I want you to place me as a seal on your arm. I want you to be there for me. I want you to take the lead. I want you to be the head.' In countless churches you will find women longing for precisely *that* from their husbands. And husbands need to pick up the challenge — the *responsibility*! Following an adult Sunday school class in which I had addressed some of these issues, a husband said to me, 'It's time to stop complaining and to take the lead.' He was talking about his marriage. He was talking about his life. He was talking about where he, his wife and family were in their relationship with God. 'It's time for me to stop complaining and it's time for me to take the lead.' Men need to be saying that. And women need to be encouraging men to do that.

The seal that binds

'Many waters cannot quench love, neither can floods drown it. If a man offered for love all the wealth of his house, he would be utterly despised' (8:7).

Seals in the Old Testament are always associated with covenants. We have examples of seals that survive to this day, either in the form of a ring that was impressed upon clay, or perhaps from Mesopotamia, cylinders that would make an impression as it was rolled on wet clay. They signified ownership and authenticity.

So, what she is saying is that love, true love, cannot be stopped. Many waters cannot quench love. Love cannot be drowned in death. Nothing can stop death. Nothing can get in its way. Nothing can nullify it. You cannot cancel it. Love should be like that. She is saying, 'There's something about love, and there's something about marriage, and there's something about covenant vows that we exchange together that's irresistible, that's unchangeable, that's irrevocable, that's resolute, that's permanent; many waters cannot quench it.'

God hates divorce. The Bible says so, 'I hate divorce' (Malachi 2:16, NASV[7]). Malachi is describing how God has refused to accept the offerings of the people, and they in turn have asked, 'Why does he not?' (2:14). The answer that God gives is: 'Because the LORD was witness between you and the wife of your youth, to whom you have been faithless, though she is your companion and your wife by covenant' (2:14). God has witnessed the covenant they had made in marriage and is indignant when they divorce.

God is present when Christians marry. That is why marriage is such a solemn occasion. 'We gather together in the presence of God and this company to join together this man and this woman in holy matrimony.'

In the *presence* of God.

'Money can't buy you love'

'Money', so The Beatles sang in the Sixties, 'can't buy me love.' But John thinks that the way to please his wife and improve his marriage is to earn more money. So he works all the hours he can, staying away from the home. And sometimes that may well be necessary — sometimes. So he is out of the house eighteen hours a day; sometimes he doesn't even come home. He offers to take those business trips that take him away over weekends. The job has consumed him, and he kids himself, 'It's all for the sake of my marriage. We'll be able to do things now that we weren't able to do before.' But they do things *without* him.

There's an episode of *The West Wing* in which Leo McGarry, the President's Chief of Staff, played by John Spencer, is in the office next to the Oval Office with the President. He's saying 'Good Night!' to the President. He's there when the President goes to bed. He's there when he gets up in the morning. In between, he goes home for a few hours. There's a scene in which McGarry opens the front door, and his wife is standing just inside the front door and there are packed suitcases standing next to her. She says to him, 'This job isn't more important than our marriage.' And he replies without a pause, 'It *is* more important than our marriage, *for now*.' He's lost her, and she gets into a cab and is gone. No job is worth losing your wife over. You want to earn some more money? Who doesn't? But not at the expense of your marriage.

Wives can drive their husbands to it by complaining about what their friends can do because their husbands earn more. And they can turn around and complain that he's never home when they try to do something about it.

Strong marriages are built on secure foundations and respect for the boundaries God has set. Committing to be a biblical spouse — a loving husband, a supportive wife — takes daily effort and focus. But the goal is breathtaking: to create a marriage in which our children might say, 'The love of Jesus is like the love my father has for my mother.' *That* is the model (cf. Ephesians 5:25-33).

It takes *grace*. And *self-denial*. And *more grace*.

Song of Solomon 8:5-14

OTHERS

5   *Who is that coming up from the wilderness,*
leaning on her beloved?

SHE

Under the apple tree I awakened you.
There your mother was in labour with you;
*   there she who bore you was in labour.*

6   *Set me as a seal upon your heart,*
*   as a seal upon your arm,*
for love is strong as death,
*   jealousy is fierce as the grave.*
Its flashes are flashes of fire,
*   the very flame of the* LORD.
7   *Many waters cannot quench love,*
*   neither can floods drown it.*
If a man offered for love
*   all the wealth of his house,*
*   he would be utterly despised.*

OTHERS/BROTHERS

8   *We have a little sister,*
        and she has no breasts.
    What shall we do for our sister
        on the day when she is spoken for?

9   *If she is a wall,*
        we will build on her a battlement of silver,
    but if she is a door,
        we will enclose her with boards of cedar.

SHE

10   *I was a wall,*
        and my breasts were like towers;
    then I was in his eyes
        as one who finds peace.

11   *Solomon had a vineyard at Baal-hamon;*
        he let out the vineyard to keepers;
        each one was to bring for its fruit a thousand pieces
            of silver.

12   *My vineyard, my very own, is before me;*
        you, O Solomon, may have the thousand,
        and the keepers of the fruit two hundred.

HE

13   *O you who dwell in the gardens,*
        with companions listening for your voice;
        let me hear it.

SHE

14   *Make haste, my beloved,*
        and be like a gazelle
    or a young stag
        on the mountains of spices.

8.

Mountains of spice

Thou art my life, my love, my heart,
The very eyes of me;
And hast command of every part,
To live and die for thee.

ROBERT HERRICK (1591–1674)

Aberystwyth! 'The principal holiday resort and administrative centre of the west coast of Wales', says a somewhat colourless web site, adding, 'It is also home to the University of Wales and the National Library.' But for this writer, it is the place where, in 1971, I met my wife Rosemary. I cannot think about the town without thinking of her. Most evenings, whatever the weather, we walked along the promenade and 'kicked the bar' at either end (a local tradition). We went to church together; attended Inter-Varsity Christian Union meetings together. Less romantically, we studied mathematics together. And we were drawn to each other. Aberystwyth brings back a flood of memories of a relationship that grew over the space of several years. She was my only true love, the only girl I ever kissed! And, in 1976, we married — in Aberystwyth, naturally!

As we think back, and we often do, we find ourselves marvelling at the providence that drew us together, me from a farm in West Wales and my wife from Belfast, Northern Ireland. 'The Troubles' (the period of violence in Northern Ireland that started in the late 1960s and lasted until the late 1990s) had caused Rosemary to consider university education on 'the mainland'. I was not a Christian and when the time for choosing universities came, I had considered going as far away as possible, but ended up choosing the university barely forty miles from where I had been raised.

Within a few months of attending the university, I was converted. And, a few months later, I met the girl who I would later marry. It was not love at first sight. I was a Christian of a few weeks standing, eager but confused, when I met Rosemary. She was a mature believer of Presbyterian convictions! If I'm honest, it was her cooking that drew me! But in time, as friendship grew to something more serious, I was drawn to consider the 'M' word — *marriage*.

How do Christians, who desire a godly marriage, go about choosing a partner? The closing poem of the Song of Solomon (8:5-14) provides some noteworthy answers.

Let your family help

In verse 8, we are introduced to the young woman's brothers — 'we have a little sister' (8:8) suggests they are brothers. Their sister 'has no breasts' (8:8), suggesting that she is still very young and unable to make decisions for herself. Where is the young girl's father? Maybe he is dead, and the brothers have taken over the responsibility of ensuring that she is properly cared for.

I jokingly sent my daughter's would-be husband a spoof 'Application for permission to date my daughter' form. It asked all kinds of questions: Do you have one male and one female parent? Do you own a truck with oversized tyres? Do you have an earring, nose ring, belly-button ring, or a tattoo? In 25 words or less, what does 'late' mean to you? In 25 words or less, what does 'don't touch my daughter' mean to you? In two words, what does 'abstinence' mean to you? And so on! It was (partly) in jest. He took it well, and they are now happily married. *With my blessing.*

Not every Christian parent makes wise choices for their children. We make bad choices for ourselves and we are equally capable of making bad choices for our children. Wanting social and monetary success for our children can be a disastrous agenda in choosing what is spiritually best for our children. Preparing our children for the mature relationships of marriage is about the most difficult thing we are asked to do as parents.

The young woman's brothers are showing concern for their sister's future as a wife and mother. They want to be sure that she marries a godly husband who will love and care for her and be a good father to their children. We find ourselves worrying that the mistakes of our own marriages might have dire consequences on our children. It is all too easy to become cynical when so many of the factors are beyond our control.

What is especially interesting about this passage is the fact that the brothers are showing concern when their sister is still young. This is not a last-minute concern when in all likelihood it is too late to change things. Their sister's thinking needs to be shaped by a godly world view while she is still young. It is the best and most formative influence they will have — ensuring that she is raised in a godly environment so that she will learn to make godly choices for herself.

Virtue matters

'If she is a wall,' they said, 'we will build on her a battlement of silver, but if she is a door, we will enclose her with boards of cedar' (v. 9). What is in view here is their sister's virtue. If she is an 'open door' — promiscuous, loose, open to whatever advances come her way, swept overboard by the good-looking senior high boy so that she's prepared to do whatever it takes to have him, or succumb to whatever pressures placed upon her by him, then the brothers are proposing drastic action. Do you understand? They are going to lock her in with planks of cedar-wood nailed to the doors and windows! They are going to lock her up!

The issue is virtue. Actually it is an issue that this young woman has been speaking to her friends about on three occasions in the course of the Song of Solomon. At moments of romantic tension, she has said to those young women, 'Do not stir up or awaken love until it pleases' (cf. 2:7; 3:5; 8:4). She has demonstrated to them her virtuous intentions.

It is about being chaste. It is about being a virgin when you marry. There is something wonderfully romantic about that. There is *nothing* more romantic than that — that your wife is the only woman you have ever known; your husband is the only man you have ever known. And this should be something we desire not only for our sisters and daughters, but also our brothers and sons. Chastity is equally a virtue for both sexes.

Listen to the young woman as she speaks. 'I was a wall,' she says (8:10). She is boasting about her chastity. She is boasting about her virtue. She is boasting about the stand that she has taken. And she is commending it to her friends.

Are you 'a wall' or are you 'a door'? Are you asking, 'Am I going to save myself for my future spouse?' What would Jesus want you to say in answer to that question? Honestly! If your answer to that question is, 'I want to be a wall. I want to be chaste; I want to be a virgin when I get married,' then promise it! And live according to that promise which you make. Hold yourself accountable to it. It says a great deal about your character how you answer that question!

God's timing is perfect

Take a look at verse 10. In the first half of the verse, she says, 'I was a wall, and my breasts were like towers.' She has grown up now, you understand. 'Then I was in his eyes as one who finds peace.' She has grown up and found the one who will be her husband. And the way she puts it brings to the surface the *timing of God*.

The word 'then' in the Hebrew is very emphatic. She has just said that she was a virgin, that she has kept herself pure. That is a stance that she had taken. She hadn't slept around. She hadn't engaged in any kind of premarital sex, and then … and then she found him. And then he found her. The implication is that she was doing what she was supposed to do, and then God did something. God in his marvellous providence brought the two of them together. 'And then…'

Singleness can be God's calling, in which case it is both good (1 Corinthians 7:1, 8, 26) and God's gift (7:7). Marriage is not God's will for everybody. Yet those who find themselves single but *long* to be married are subject to a variety of temptations. It is not easy to be single when God has not given the gift of singleness. The temptation then arises to *run ahead* of the providence of God.

This is what Naomi did. I have no doubt whatsoever that she loved her daughter-in-law deeply. But when she suggested to Ruth that she should go, perfumed, to where Boaz lay sleeping, in the middle of the night, 'uncover his feet' and lie there until morning, it had folly written all over it. No amount of contextualization (and there is much of it to be done) can rid the story of the charge that Naomi was trying to bring about something *by her own efforts and scheming*. It was only because Boaz was a godly man that Ruth's honour was still intact when morning dawned. It is apparent that Boaz understood the danger all too well, not so much for himself but from the gossip that would ensue when he charges his men, 'Let it not be known that the woman came to the threshing floor' (Ruth 3:14).

The young woman in the Song of Solomon met her husband at work. Verses 11 and 12 are a little complicated, but essentially she is saying that she was working in a vineyard, gathering grapes, when she first saw him. God brought it about. She met her future husband in the course of the *ordinary* providence of God. She wasn't doing something unusual.

This is meant to encourage us to think that, ordinarily, God will guide us in the course of our daily obedience to our duty. That may sound terribly unromantic, but it is wonderfully reassuring to know that God can be trusted to provide for us without our having to perform something extraordinary to bring it about. That is not God's way in every instance, of course, but it is what happened here. 'I've been trusting him,' you might be saying. Then do not stop trusting him. 'Delight yourself in the LORD, and he will give you the desires of your heart' (Psalm 37:4).

The way she puts it is meant to signify that she found in the young man something she had already grown to love even before she met him. 'I was in his eyes as one who finds peace' (8:10). The Hebrew may signify a nuance that fails to come across in the English text. She found 'peace' (*shalom*) in his eyes. It almost sounds as though her words are meant to remind us of Noah finding *grace* in the eyes of the Lord (cf. Genesis 6:8). In this case, it is *peace* in the eyes of the man. When the two of them met, there was a sense of peace. There was a sense of 'this is how it ought to be' about it. There was a sense of fulfilment. This is how she had expected it to be. There was a sense of the providence of God in it. What a beautiful way to start a marriage: waiting patiently on God's time!

The whole is greater than the sum of the parts

When these two met and fell in love, they found peace in each other's eyes; they completed each other. Do you remember how in the book of Genesis, Eve is described as Adam's *helper* (cf. Genesis 2:20)? Together, Adam and Eve were far greater than the sum of their individual contribution; together as husband and wife, as a unity, they were far greater than they would ever have been individually. The *shalom* of their relationship was evocative of something profound.

This is the greatest test of a marriage. Is this a person in whose companionship I will grow and become something that I could never be on my own? The Christian psychologist, William Kilpatrick, citing C. S. Lewis, says, 'We are one vast need.'[1] Our intuitive feeling when we are in love is that before this moment, we were only half-alive! It is a humbling, and for some a disturbing, thought that much of our wholeness depends on someone outside of ourselves. Take away the love of our lives and we feel reduced to almost nothing.

Marriages are built on communication

At the end of the Song of Solomon, the time for reminiscing seems over; they are now speaking to each other. He says to her, '...your voice; let me hear it' (8:13).

Before I was married, I would lie awake at night, thinking of the conversations I had had that evening with my fiancé. I couldn't wait to be with her again, and pick up on the conversation. I remember long telephone calls during university holidays when we were parted. And when she began teaching in a High School several hours away from where I lived, the silence was painful. Couples are meant to *talk*. And couples who love each other talk to each other.

Marriages tend to unravel when couples stop talking to each other. What conversations there are seem to consist of barked orders and minimal necessary information. They have found someone *else* who listens to them, someone who understands them. A secretary. A friend at church. And trouble is sure to follow.

A good sign of where our marriage might be is whether I still thrill to hear the voice of the one I love. Is there some self-examination to do in this regard? Is there some repentance to engage in? Some husbands may attempt self-justification by saying, 'But that's the way I am.' But that is *not* the way that you were when you were courting your wife! *Then*, you longed to hear her every word!

Good marriages need nurturing

The young woman says something wonderfully romantic in the closing verse:

> Make haste, my beloved,
>   and be like a gazelle
> or a young stag
>   on the mountains of spices

(8:14).

'Hurry home!' is what she is saying. Specifically, the verb is 'Flee!', but we could easily draw the wrong conclusion. She wants him to flee from where he is and return to her. She wants him to come home.

She wants him to come to 'the mountain of spices'. We've come across these 'spices' before. Her perfume (4:10) and her 'garden' (4:12-16; 5:1; 6:2) are of spice. His cheeks are like beds of spices (5:13). She wants them to be together. Alone! It's the point at which, at least in older movies, the camera panned wide and the lights faded and the music played.

We have looked at the Song of Solomon as a love song between a man and a woman. It is has been about romance, about sexuality, about marriage. It has also been about growing in love for one another. And the desires that end the book — 'the mountain of spices' — is, in the end, about the joy of togetherness. And the freshness will be maintained so long as one sees in the other the beauty that lasts — the beauty of godliness that reflects the eternal beauty of Jesus Christ.

The best marriages are the ones that put Jesus Christ first.

Oh, Lord our God, our homes are thine forever!
We trust to thee their problems, toil and care;
their bonds of love no enemy can sever,
if thou art always Lord and Master there:
be thou the center of our least endeavor,
be thou our guests, our hearts and homes to share.

Barbara Hart (1965)

The Song ends in a longing for consummation but one that isn't actually expressed. The yearning is perhaps a poetic description of how, even in marriage and sexual union, there is still something that remains incomplete, unfulfilled. The longing remains even though a temporary pleasure has been achieved.

It is, in its own way, a signal that the pleasures of this life, rich and rewarding as they are, are never fully satisfying. The joy of union with another is but a pale reflection of the joy of union with the resurrected Lord.

Only 'in Christ' are we 'complete' (Colossians 2:10, AV).

Appendix

Interpreting the Song of Solomon

Writing a book based on Solomon's[1] poems is bound to be troublesome. The Westminster Assembly censured interpreters who have 'received it as a hot, carnal pamphlet formed by some loose Apollo or Cupid'.[2] In an attempt to placate the rise of Platonism in the early third century, Origen, along with Clement, his predecessor in Alexandria, suggested that the Bible (especially the Old Testament) should be read *allegorically*. Every text, he taught, has its plain meaning (which is sometimes erroneous and immoral!), but also works as a parable, and then, more importantly, as a passageway to otherwise secret codes encased in mystical symbolism.

Origen's celebrated commentary on the Song of Songs[3] is a case in point. In its admittedly 'erotic' verse, he found a wealth of meditation on the union between Christ and the church. This enabled him to marry Christianity and Platonism and promote a deity 'ever unmoved and untroubled in his own summit of bliss'[4] as an acceptable notion to both sides. When Jerome came to write a preface to Origen's sermons on the Song of Solomon, his motto being *omnis coitus impurus* (basically, 'all sex is impure'), he assured those who kept themselves free from sexual defilement that they would be rewarded by Jesus their bridegroom. Trouble has ensued ever since!

My own understanding of the Song of Solomon has changed with time. Thirty-five years ago, I heard the late William Still give a series of four marvellous addresses at (what was then) the Inter-Varsity Fellowship's student retreat in Bryntirion (in South Wales). It was a *tour de force* of Christ-centred preaching and teaching in the allegorical style. There were a lot of quotations from the *Westminster Confession*, and an assurance that the Song was an allegory of the relationship of Christ to the church. There was abundant passion in what he said; but he did not fully persuade. Then came my own call to ministry and twenty years of preaching passed by with never a sermon on the Song. True, tangential allusions were made employing references to the 'lilies of the valley' and 'fairer than ten thousand' and the like;[5] but absolutely no hint of the 'erotic' that undergirds these references.

Call it a hangover of Victorianism, or a sheltered upbringing in the hills of West Wales, but sermons on courtship, sex and marriage were not in my repertoire; until, that is, I moved to the United States in the mid 1990s. I recall an elder once saying, hinting at a biblical reference to Nazareth, that no good thing ever comes out of America, and the idea that the Song of Solomon was first and foremost about romance and sexuality — a majority view in conservative churches these days in America — would have only confirmed his prejudice had he lived long enough to hear me suggest it! The truth is, even if we admit that the analogy of Christ's relationship to the church as a bridegroom wooing his bride is a biblical one (*and it is!*), the fact of the matter remains that for this analogy to mean anything, the underlying issue to which it is a parallel must equally be true, otherwise the analogy is based in fiction.

Genre

The Song of Solomon, along with the Psalms, Proverbs and Ecclesiastes, is one of the *wisdom* books of the Old Testament.

Appendix

By 'wisdom literature' we generally mean books that teach us how we may live in the practical affairs of everyday life to the glory of God. Solomon writes in Ecclesiastes that there is 'a time to embrace, and a time to refrain from embracing' (Ecclesiastes 3:5). The Song of Solomon deals with the former: times when it is appropriate to embrace. It gives us a picture of a man and a woman who are passionately in love and who marry and embrace. It tells a story, common enough to the course of love, that spells complication and dénouement. Obstacles and rivals have to be overcome. Trust has to be forged. Disappointment and suspicions have to be overcome. The course of true love (in a fallen world, at least) never did run smooth.

In the Hebrew Bible the order of the wisdom literature is different from our English Bible, and the Song of Solomon comes *before* Ecclesiastes. The order is as follows: Proverbs, Ruth, Song of Songs and Ecclesiastes. The book of Proverbs ends with a picture of the ideal woman, the virtuous woman (cf. Proverbs 31:10-31). Ruth gives us an *example* of a virtuous woman. And the Song of Solomon continues with a virtuous woman who marries her ideal husband.

Style and interpretation

The style of the Song of Solomon is distinctive among the wisdom literature, for it is a book of poetry — *Hebrew* poetry. By the end of the first century, the church had more or less separated entirely from the synagogue. Various parties were emerging calling into question the relationship of the church to the Old Testament Scriptures. However solid the Hebrew canon was to the Jews, its relationship to the New Testament church was a matter of growing debate, especially a book as peculiar as the Song of Solomon. To sections of the church already beginning to be influenced by Platonic ideas which devalued the flesh, its eroticism was unacceptable.

Following the destruction of Jerusalem and its temple in AD 70, and along with it the demise of the powerful Sanhedrin court, the Jewish power base moved to the 'college of Jabneh'. It was here that the roots of the literature of Jewish tradition — Midrash and Mishnah, Talmud and Aggadah — were nourished and strengthened. At the Council of Jamnia in AD 90, a small gathering of rabbinic Jewish leaders gathered *not to discuss or 'fix' the Old Testament canon* as is often suggested; that canon had been settled before the birth of Jesus in Bethlehem! Debate, however, did take place on the reason why 'difficult' books like the Song of Solomon and Ecclesiastes were seen as bearing inherent canonical status. Rabbi Akiba, one of the prominent names in that council, insisted on interpreting the Song allegorically, thereby lessening some of the objections that were then current over its contents. If all the sacred writings are holy, then this one, he argued, is the holy of holies; but he added that it should not be read in public to those under thirty!

Since that time, Christians, too, have asked similar questions. Specifically, is the Song a book about human relationships and, in particular, human sexuality? Or, is it an extended allegory, like the story of the cave of shadowy representations in Plato's *Republic*, or similar tales in Ovid's *Metamorphoses*, or the more familiar tale of Christian fleeing the City of Destruction in John Bunyan's *Pilgrim's Progress*? Are the characters and life situations in the Song of Solomon meant to be reflective of something else or *someone* else: the love of Jesus for the Church? Is the book meant to teach us how to love Jesus? Or how he loves us? Or both? And is one more dominant than the other? And if so, which one?

As we have already seen, by the third century, Platonism (or neo-Platonism) was on the rise and Origen in Alexandria (perhaps the most important city next to Rome at the time) managed to avoid wholesale rejection of the Song by suggesting that its primary meaning was an allegorical one.

Appendix

Bernard of Clairvaux (1090-1153), who preached a series of eighty-six sermons on the Song of Solomon, understood the theme of the book to teach that true love 'seeking its source again … will always draw afresh from it'.[6] In the opening verses of the Song, Bernard sees a reference to something more than kissing; what the kiss represents is the union of the divine and human in the incarnation of Jesus Christ, the God-man. For Bernard, there is a significant reason why the Song begins with the request to be kissed 'with the kisses of his mouth' rather than 'with his mouth'. The latter is appropriate only for 'the Word who assumes human nature'. He explains:

> It is for this reason that none of the saints dared say: 'let him kiss me with his mouth', but rather, 'with the kiss of his mouth'. In this way they paid tribute to that prerogative of Christ, on whom uniquely and in one sole instance the mouth of the Word was pressed, that moment when the fullness of the divinity yielded itself to him as the life of his body. A fertile kiss therefore, a marvel of stupendous self-abasement that is not a mere pressing of mouth upon mouth; it is the uniting of God with man. Normally the touch of lip on lip is the sign of the loving embrace of hearts, but this conjoining of natures brings together the human and divine, shows God reconciling 'to himself all things whether on earth or in heaven'.[7]

Bernard sincerely held the conviction that despite the graphic anatomical and sensual allusions, it is still possible to confine our thoughts to the spiritual relationship the believer enjoys with Christ.

We can span half a millennium from Bernard, and an entire millennium from Origen and find that hardly anything has changed. In sixteenth-century Geneva, John Calvin held essentially the same view, though arriving at it from a different exegetical path to Origen.

The Puritans adopted this allegorical interpretation. Possibly, the world had not seen such enthusiastic preaching on the Song since the days of Origen. One of the great commentaries on the Song of Solomon was written by the seventeenth-century Scottish preacher, James Durham. In his 'Key Useful' — the introduction to the commentary — Durham explains his interpretive procedure:

> This Song is not to be taken properly ... or literally, that is, as the words do at first sound; but it is to be taken and understood spiritually, figuratively and allegorically, as having some Spiritual meaning contained under these figurative expressions, made use of throughout this Song: My meaning is, that when it speaketh of a Marriage, Spouse, Sister, Beloved, Daughters of Jerusalem &c., these expressions are not to be understood properly of such, but as holding forth something of a Spiritual Nature under these.[8]

In the late nineteenth century, C. H. Spurgeon identified fifty-seven Puritan commentaries on the Song of Solomon, all of which he commends! Among them, Spurgeon highlights one by Richard Sibbes, written in 1639, entitled *Discovery of the Near and Dear Love, Union and Communion Between Christ and the Church*, and one by the famous Baptist systematic theologian, John Gill, *An Exposition of the book of Solomon's Song*. Spurgeon adds that 'one who despises it is incapable of elevated spiritual feelings'. And in one by John Collinge, written in 1676, *Intercourses of Divine Love Between Christ and His Church Metaphorically Expressed by Solomon in Canticles 1 and 2*, there are 999 pages that only cover the first two chapters of the Song of Solomon.[9]

Appendix

In Jonathan Edwards' *Personal Narrative*, looking back to his late teenage period and his experience of conversion as a teenager, he speaks of a verse in the Song of Solomon that he remembers: 'I am the rose of Sharon and the lily of the valleys' (Song of Solomon 2:1).[10]

Edwards comments:

> The words seemed to me sweetly to represent the loveliness and beauty of Jesus Christ. The whole book of Song of Songs used to be pleasant to me, and I used to be much in reading of it, about that time; and found from time to time an inward sweetness, that would carry me away in my contemplations.[11]

Few have captured the essence of the *poetry* of the Song of Solomon as Anne Bradstreet. Sixty years of age and dying of a painful disease, she wrote 'As Weary Pilgrim'. In a climactic moment, looking forward to the consummation of all things, Bradstreet reflects on her union with Jesus Christ and took hold of some thoughts from the Song of Solomon:

> Lord make me ready for that day;
> Then, Come deare bridgrome. Come away.

The allegorical tradition continues almost unabated in our time, particularly among those of a reformed persuasion. In addition to the re-publication of older commentaries, allegorical approaches to the Song of Solomon continue to be written, with considerable skill and insight.[12] Even so, there are signs that the tide of interpretive opinion may be changing. Significant exegetical commentaries have emerged[13] suggesting that a fresh look at this book is in order.

Love poetry

Such a 'fresh look' begins by emphasizing that the Song is *love poetry*. Strictly, it is *lyric* poetry, finding parallels in Egyptian love poetry. Since the subject matter is monogamous marital love, it is not inappropriate that the canon of Scripture contain examples of the language of love. Since the Bible affirms the essential goodness of the physical universe, including the physical body, denouncing as error attempts at defining true spirituality in non-material forms, it is perfectly proper that the canon contains material expressing human sexuality. It does so with profound and moving suggestion, but avoids the lurid and titillating.

Furthermore, more accurately the Song is a *collection* of poems; and it depends upon which commentary you are reading as to how many poems it contains — some see seven and others twenty-three! Michael Travers explains its significance:

Poetry is more intense than prose; it's briefer than prose. It has rhythm; it uses physical objects as symbols. Love involves the emotions and senses as well as the mind. Prose relies on the sequence of words to develop a logical statement. Prose can't capture love's immediacy and urgency. In short, poetry says a great deal in a few words and it does so intensely. When we have intense emotion, we need to express it in physical terms. Poetry does that for us. Poetry is more than pretty language. It expresses the depth and breadth of love more completely than prose. Another factor in poetry is that it demands a response from its reader; it is written to someone in particular, whereas prose is written to a generic audience. In love poetry, the reader becomes the loved one. Whether or not we like it, we are forced to respond. The love poetry in the Song of Songs involves us emotionally as well as intellectually. We cannot dismiss it.[14]

Appendix

I have always been keenly fond of Shakespeare's *Sonnets*. Written in the early seventeenth century, these 154 sonnets comprise a high point in English literature. Number 18 is often cited:

> Shall I compare thee to a summer's day?
> Thou art more lovely and more temperate.
> Rough winds do shake the darling buds of May,
> And summer's leaves have all too short a date.
> Sometime too hot the eye of heaven shines,
> And often is his gold complexion dimmed.

But would-be lovers should try these lines instead:

> Behold, you are beautiful, my love…
> Your hair is like a flock of goats…
> Your teeth are like a flock of shorn ewes
>   that have come up from the washing,
> all of which bear twins,
>   and not one among them has lost its young…
> Your cheeks are like halves of a pomegranate
>   behind your veil.
> Your neck is like the tower of David,
>   built in rows of stone.
>
> (Song of Solomon 4:1-3)

For this lover, what attracts is the fact that she possesses all her teeth! Or perhaps, my favourite:

> Your nose is like a tower of Lebanon,
>   which looks towards Damascus.
>
> (Song of Solomon 7:4)

Clearly, beauty is in the eye of the beholder!

Author

A problem remains over the human author. Despite the many references to Solomon (1:1, 5; 3:7, 9, 11; 8:11, 12), nowhere does it state that he is the author. Even so, the allusion to Solomon, as the archetypal lover, is in itself problematic. True, he knew as well as anyone the subtleties of relating to the opposite sex, and no doubt can teach some things about the language of courtship and sexuality. But, how can someone who had 'seven hundred wives' (1 Kings 11:3) teach us anything about a monogamous relationship?

To be technical, the Hebrew for the phrase 'of Solomon' is the *lahmed*, which can mean many things, but it does not necessarily imply that everything comes from the pen of Solomon. Perhaps, all that it means is that it was Solomonic, that is, it belonged to that group of literature that was regarded as wisdom literature, and was generally spoken of as the wisdom of Solomon.

Solomon did have one favourite wife, the daughter of the Pharaoh of Egypt; but this appears to have been for political expediency more than anything else.

For further study

Brady, Gary. *Heavenly Love: The Song of Solomon Simply Explained*, Welwyn Commentary Series, Darlington: Evangelical Press, 2006. Takes a middle ground between the literal and allegorical interpretations.

Burrowes, George. *A Commentary on the Song of Solomon*, Edinburgh: Banner of Truth, 1973. Allegorical interpretation.

Carr, Lloyd G. *The Song of Solomon: An Introduction and Commentary*, The Tyndale Old Testament Commentaries, Leicester: IVP, 1984. A concise commentary that follows a 'natural' or 'literal' interpretation.

Appendix

Durham, James. *An Exposition of the Song of Solomon*, Edinburgh: Banner of Truth, 1982. A classic allegorical interpretation of the Song of Solomon written by the great Scottish divine.

Ellsworth, Roger. *He Is Altogether Lovely: Discovering Christ in the Song of Solomon,* Darlington: Evangelical Press, 1998. Allegorical interpretation.

Fortner, Don. *Discovering Christ in the Song of Solomon,* Darlington: Evangelical Press, 2005. Allegorical interpretation.

Garrett, Duane. *Song of Solomon & Ecclesiastes*, Word Biblical Commentary, Vol. 23B, Nashville, TN: Thomas Nelson Publishers, 2004. Adopts a 'literal' approach in a format that is not always accessible.

Gledhill, T. *The Message of Song of Songs*, Bible Speaks Today, Leicester: IVP, 1994. Follows a non-allegorical interpretation.

Glickman, S. Craig. *A Song for Lovers*, Eugene, Oregon: Wipf and Stock Publishers, 2002. An excellent and accessible non-allegorical commentary, including a helpful section on interpreting the Song of Solomon. Another edition of this work, *Solomon's Song of Love: Let a Song of Songs inspire your own Romantic Story,* has since appeared, but contains some generally unhelpful material. The reference here is to the 2002 edition.

Hess, Richard S. *Song of Songs*, Grand Rapids: Baker Academic, 2005.

Knight, George A. *Revelation of Love: A Commentary on The Song of Songs*, International Theological Commentary, Grand Rapids: Eerdmans, 1988. A brief introduction to the Song of Songs as a 'collection of love poems'.

Longman III, Tremper. *Song of Songs*, The New International Commentary on the Old Testament, Grand Rapids: Eerdmans, 2001. A more critical and exegetical study of Song of Songs.

Provan, Iain. *Ecclesiastes, Song of Songs*, The NIV Application Commentary, Grand Rapids: Zondervan, 2001. A homiletical exposition that interprets Song of Songs as a developing 'drama' of a male-female relationship.

Notes

Chapter 1

1. Charles Williams, *He Came Down From Heaven* (Heinemann, 1938), 90.

Chapter 2

1. Matthew Henry, *Matthew Henry's Commentary on the Whole Bible* (USA: Hendrickson, 1991), 1:16. These comments were originally those of Peter Lombard's. See p.96.

Chapter 3

1. Jonathan Edwards, *The Works of Jonathan Edwards*, 22 volumes to date, eds Perry Miller, John E. Smith, Harry S. Stout; Vol. 13 'The Miscellanies' (New Haven: Yale University Press, 1957-), 13:278, cf. Jonathan Edwards, 'A Dissertation Concerning The Nature of True Virtue', *Works*, 1:122-142, especially p.128.
2. Edwards, *Works* (Banner of Truth edition in 2 vols), 1:xxxvi.

Chapter 4

1. The identification of the speakers is conjectural and commentators differ widely. Some attribute 3:6-11 to the young woman, but the opening sentence at 3:6 'What is that...' is in the feminine suggesting that this is the young man speaking.
2. C. S. Lewis, *Mere Christianity* (New York: Touchstone, 1996), 91-92.
3. Eudaimonism is a word derived from the Greek for 'well-being' and connotes a philosophy that defines right action as that which leads to well-being. The concept originates in Aristotle's *Nichomachean Ethics*.

Notes

Chapter 7

1. This section belongs to a larger section, or poem: 8:5-14. The poem as a whole will be considered in the next chapter.
2. The (Hebrew) Masoretic text understands that the woman is speaking here. This makes an allegorical reading of the passage impossible. How can Israel or the church, the female, awaken Yahweh or Christ, the male? The Syriac switched the gender and allegorical interpretations followed suit. For an extended discussion, see Richard S. Hess, *Song of Songs*, 237.
3. Cited by Stuart B. Babbage, *Christianity and Sex* (Chicago, IL: InterVarsity, 1963), 10.
4. George Marsden, *Jonathan Edwards, A Life* (New Haven & London: Yale University Press, 2003), 101, 107.
5. Henry-Louis de la Grange, *Guatav Mahler. Vienna: The Years of Challenge (1897-1904)* (Oxford, New York: Oxford University Press, 1995), 450.
6. *National Review* (16 June 2003): 6, cited in *Does Christianity Squash Women: A Christian Looks at Womanhood*, by Rebecca Jones (Nashville, TN: Broadman & Holman, 2005), 2.
7. The ESV translates this differently, 'For the man who hates and divorces, says the LORD, the God of Israel, covers his garment with violence...', but offers the alternative translation, 'For the LORD, the God of Israel, says that he hates divorce, and him who covers...'

Chapter 8

1. Cited by Rodney Clapp, 'What Hollywood doesn't know about romantic love', at http://www.christianitytoday.com/ct/2001/107/31.0.html (20 July 2006).

Appendix

1. Solomon is mentioned several times (1:1, 5; 3:7, 9, 11; 8:11, 12), but authorship is never attributed to him.
2. Westminster Assembly, *Annotations Upon All the Books of the Old and New Testaments* (London, 1651), Vol. 1 (no pagination), cited by William Phipps in *Recovering Biblical Sensuousness* (Philadelphia: The Westminster Press, 1975), 58. Earlier, Phipps cites Jerome's instruction 'that a girl should not study the book until other studies were completed', since 'she might be harmed by not perceiving that it was the song of a spiritual wedding expressed in fleshly language'. Op. cit., 52.

3. For a 'modern' edition, see Origen, *The Song of Songs, Commentary and Homilies*, trans. and ed. by R. P. Lawson, Ancient Christian Writers Series, Vol. 26 (Paulist Press, 1957).

4. Origen, *Homilies on Numbers*, 33:2, in Henry Bettenson, *The Early Christian Fathers* (London: Oxford University Press, 1956), 187.

5. Cf. Song of Songs 2:1; 5:10.

6. *Bernard of Clairvaux: On The Song of Songs* (4 vols.), Vol. 4 , trans. by Kilian Walsh (Kalamazoo, MI: Cistercian Publications, 1981), Sermon 83:4, 184.

7. *Ibid*. Vol. 1, Sermon 2:2, 10.

8. James Durham, *An Exposition of the Song of Solomon* (Edinburgh: Banner of Truth, [1849], 1989), 27-28.

9. C. H. Spurgeon, *Commenting and Commentaries* (Edinburgh: Banner of Truth, [1876] 1969), 113. Spurgeon adds the comment to the volume by Collinge, 'Nine hundred and nine quarto pages upon one chapter is more than enough... It would try the constitutions of many modern divines to read what these Puritans found it a pleasure to write.' *Ibid.*, 112.

10. Arguably, however, it is not the man but the woman who speaks these words, and making this a description of Jesus Christ (as Edwards does and others since) is problematic.

11. 'Memoirs of Jonathan Edwards', in *The Works of Jonathan Edwards*, 2 vols. (Edinburgh: Banner of Truth, 1974), 1:xiii.

12. See, for example, Don Fortner, *Discovering Christ in the Song of Solomon* (Darlington: Evangelical Press, 2005); Roger Ellsworth, *He Is Altogether Lovely: Discovering Christ in the Song of Solomon* (Darlington: Evangelical Press, 1998). The commentary by Gary Brady, *Heavenly Love: The Song of Solomon Simply Explained*, Welwyn Commentary Series (Darlington: Evangelical Press, 2006) takes a middle approach between the allegorical and the literal interpretation. Note the comment of Duane Garrett who cites J. R. R. Tolkien's 1936 lecture on *Beowulf* in which he protests about those who read (and criticize) *The Beowulf* 'as a quarry of fact and fancy far more assiduously than it has been studied as a work of art'. Garrett adds, 'Much the same is true of the study of the Song.' Word Biblical Commentary 23B, *Song of Solomon & Lamentations* (Nashville: Thomas Nelson Publishers, 2004), 14.

13. The commentaries by Hess, Longman, Provan and Garrett, especially. See list of books for further study, pp.124-5.

14. In an e-mail to me in 2005.